AQA GCSE History

D1613074

HEALTH AND THE PEOPLE

Alf Wilkinson

Approval message from AQA

This textbook has been approved by AQA for use with our qualification. This means that we have checked that it broadly covers the specification and we are satisfied with the overall quality. Full details of our approval process can be found on our website.

We approve textbooks because we know how important it is for teachers and students to have the right resources to support their teaching and learning. However, the publisher is ultimately responsible for the editorial control and quality of this book.

Please note that when teaching the **AQA GCSE History** course, you must refer to AQA's specification as your definitive source of information. While this book has been written to match the specification, it cannot provide complete coverage of every aspect of the course.

A wide range of other useful resources can be found on the relevant subject pages of our website: www.aqa.org.uk.

DYNAMIC LEARNING

HODDER EDUCATION
AN HACHETTE UK COMPANY

Orders: please contact Bookpoint Ltd, 130 Park Drive, Milton Park, Abingdon, Oxon OX14 4SE. Telephone: (44) 01235 827720. Fax: (44) 01235 400454. Email education@bookpoint. co.uk Lines are open from 9 a.m. to 5 p.m., Monday to Saturday, with a 24-hour message answering service. You can also order through our website: www.hoddereducation.co.uk

ISBN: 9781471864216

© Alf Wilkinson 2016

First published in 2016 by

Hodder Education,

An Hachette UK Company

Carmelite House

50 Victoria Embankment

London EC4Y 0DZ

www.hoddereducation.co.uk

Impression number 10 9 8 7 6 5 4 3

Year   2019 2018 2017

Cover photo © H. ARMSTRONG ROBERTS/Corbis

Illustrations by Aptara, Integra, Barking Dog Art and Tony Randell

Typeset by Melissa Brunelli Design

Printed in Dubai

A catalogue record for this title is available from the British Library.

CONTENTS

Health and the People

ACKNOWLEDGEMENTS

The Publishers would like to thank Ian Dawson for his contributions to the Medical Moments in Time features on pages 22–23, 38–39, 64–65, 90–91

The Publishers would like to thank the following for permission to reproduce copyright material.

Picture credits

p.1 *t* © Jochen Sands/DigitalVision/Thinkstock, *c* © Justin Kase zsixz/Alamy Stock Photo, *b* © Martin Siepmann/Getty Images; **p.4** © Georgios Kollidas/iStock/Thinkstock; **p.6** © Okea/iStock/Thinkstock; **p.7** The Black Death (gouache on paper), Nicolle, Pat (Patrick) (1907-95)/Private Collection/© Look and Learn/Bridgeman Images; **p.8** © Dmitry Kalinovsky/123RF; **p.11** © British Library/Robana/REX Shutterstock; **p.15** *l* © British Library/Robana/REX Shutterstock, *r* © INTERFOTO/Alamy Stock Photo; **p.16** *t* © British Library/Robana/REX Shutterstock; *c* © Wellcome Library, London/Rare Books/http://creativecommons.org/licenses/by/4.0/, *b* Sheila Terry/Science Photo Library; **p.17** Ms Hunter 112 f.1v Arderne in the Herb Garden, from 'Incerti Avctoris' by Johannis Arderne (vellum), English School, (14th century) © Glasgow University Library, Scotland/Bridgeman Images; **p.18** Window depicting St John of Bridlington (stained glass), English School, (15th century)/ © Collegiate Church of St. Mary, Warwick, UK/Bridgeman Images; **p.19** © Wellcome Library, London/http://creativecommons.org/licenses/by/4.0/; **p.20** © Hulton Archive/GettyImages; **p.21** © Wellcome Library, London/http://creativecommons.org/licenses/by/4.0/; **p.24** © Hulton Archive/Getty Images; **p.25** © North Wind Picture Archives/Alamy Stock Photo; **p.27** © Niday Picture Library/Alamy Stock Photo; **p.32** *t* © Mary Evans Picture Library/Alamy Stock Photo, *b* © Mary Evans Picture Library/Alamy Stock Photo; **p.33** © FineArt/Alamy Stock Photo; **p.34** *l* © Photos.com/Thinkstock, *r* © Wellcome Library, London/http://creativecommons.org/licenses/by/4.0/; **p.35** © GeorgiosArt/Thinkstock; **p.36** *t* © Wellcome Library, London/http://creativecommons.org/licenses/by/4.0/, *b* © Science Photo Library/Science Photo Library; **p.41** © World History Archive/Alamy Stock Photo; **p.42** *t* © Iconographic Collections/Wellcome Library, London/http://creativecommons.org/licenses/by/4.0/, *b* © PARIS PIERCE/Alamy Stock Photo; **p.43** © Wellcome Library, London/http://creativecommons.org/licenses/by/4.0/; **p.44** © Steve Sack, courtesy of Cagle Cartoons; **p.46** *r* © Everett Collection Historical/Alamy Stock Photo Reportage/Archival image; **p.47** © INTERFOTO/Alamy Stock Photo; **p.48** © Wellcome Library, London/http://creativecommons.org/licenses/by/4.0/; **p.55** *l* © Photos.com/Thinkstock, *c* © PRISMA ARCHIVO/Alamy Stock Photo, *r* © Photos.com/Thinkstock Photos; **p.56** *t* © Chronicle/Alamy Stock Photo, *b* © H. Bedford Lemere/English Heritage/Arcaid/Corbis; **p.57** © Allister Mackrell/Alamy Stock Photo; **p.58** Advertisement for 'Brain Salt', 1890s (colour litho), English School, (19th century)/Private Collection/© The Advertising Archives/Bridgeman Images; **p.60** *t* © Pictorial Press Ltd/Alamy Stock Photo, *b* © Chronicle/Alamy Stock Photo; **p.61** *l* © Wellcome Library, London/http://creativecommons.org/licenses/by/4.0/, *r* © Science Photo Library; **p.62** *t* © Photos.com/Thinkstock, *b* © Pictorial Press Ltd/Alamy Stock Photo; **p.66** *b* © Pictorial Press Ltd/Alamy Stock Photo; **p.67** *r* © Wellcome Library, London/http://creativecommons.org/licenses/by/4.0/; **p.69** © Mary Evans Picture Library; **p.70** *b* © Bob Thomas/Popperfoto/Getty Images; **p.76** Image created by Church Action on Poverty, www.church-poverty.org.uk; **p.77** *t* © Pictorial Press Ltd/Alamy Stock Photo, *b* © Science and Society/Superstock; **p.78** Courtesy of Cartoonstock.com; **p.80** © Jean Williamson/Alamy Stock Photo; **p.82** © SSPL/Getty Images; **p.83** © World History Archive/Alamy Stock Photo; **p.84** © Keith Brofsky/Photodisc/Thinkstock; **p.85** © Permission of Cathy Wilcox, Sydney Morning Herald; **p.86** *l* © Illustrated London News Ltd/Mary Evans, *r* © The Art Archive/Alamy Stock Photo; **p.88** *t* © World History Archive/Alamy Stock Photo, *b* © Mary Evans/The National Archives, London, England; **p.89** © Popperfoto/Getty Images; **p.92** © RDImages/Epics/Getty Images; **p.93** © palatiaphoto/Alamy Stock Photo; **p.95** *l* © The National Library of Medicine, *r* © Lawkeeper/Alamy Stock Vector; **p.99** *l* © PRISMA ARCHIVO/Alamy Stock Photo, *r* © World History Archive/Alamy Stock Photo; **p.102** *tl* The Black Death (gouache on paper), Nicolle, Pat (Patrick) (1907–95)/Private Collection/© Look and Learn/Bridgeman Images, *cl* © Niday Picture Library/Alamy Stock Photo, *c* © Jean Williamson/Alamy Stock Photo, *r* © Lawkeeper/Alamy Stock Vector; **p.106** © Sheila Terry/Science Photo Library.

Text acknowledgements

p.19, Source 2: quoted from http://www.medievalists.net/2013/08/04/medieval-medical-experiments/; **p.36**, Source 3: quoted in Nathan Belofsky, *Strange Medicine* (Perigree Books, 2013), pp.45–46; **p.37**, Source 1: quoted in Mark Jackson, *The History of Medicine: A Beginner's Guide* (OneWorld Publications, 2014), pp.96–97; **p. 40**, Source 3: Joan Lane, *The Making of the 'English Patient': A Guide to Sources for the Social History of Medicine* (Sutton Publishing, 2000), p.3; **p.63**, Source 5: quoted in Roy Porter, *The Greatest Benefit to Mankind* (Fontana Press, 1999), p.373; **p.64**, Source 1: population figures from Whitaker's Almanac, 1941 (J. Whitaker & Sons, 1941); **p.78**, Source 2: quoted in Roy Porter, *The Greatest Benefit to Mankind* (Fontana Press, 1999), p.669; **p.81**, Source 2: *A Nurse at the Front – the First World War Diaries of Sister Edith Appleton* (Simon & Schuster, 2013).

HOW THIS BOOK WILL HELP YOU IN AQA GCSE HISTORY

a) It will help you to learn the content

Is your main worry when you prepare for an exam that you won't know enough to answer the questions? Many people feel that way – particularly when a course covers nearly 1,000 years of history! And it is true, you will need good knowledge of the main events and the detail to do well in this thematic study. This book will help you acquire both the overview and the detail!

The **author text** explains the key content clearly. It helps you understand each period and each topic, and the themes that connect the topics.

Diagrams and **timelines** help you to visualise and remember topics. We also encourage you to draw your own diagrams – an even better way to learn.

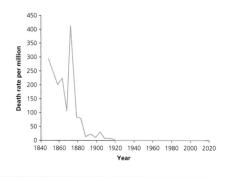

The book is full of **sources**. This course deals with some big issues and sources help pin those issues down. History is at its best when you can see what real people said, did, wrote, sang, watched, laughed about or cried over. Sources can really help you understand the story better and remember it because they help you to see the big concepts and ideas in terms of what they meant to people at the time.

SOURCE 5

Berkeley Moyniham recalls his days as a student in Leeds in the 1880s. From *The Greatest Benefit to Mankind* by Roy Porter (Fontana Press, 1999), p.373

The surgeon arrived and threw off his jacket to avoid getting blood or pus on it. He rolled up his shirt sleeves and, in the corridor to the operation room, took an ancient frock from a cupboard; it bore signs of a chequered past, and was utterly stiff with old blood. One of these coats was worn with special pride, indeed joy, as it had belonged to a retired member of staff. The cuffs were rolled up to only just above the wrists, and the hands were washed in a sink. Once clean they were rinsed in carbolic-acid solution.

SOURCE 3
A wound-man, 1517

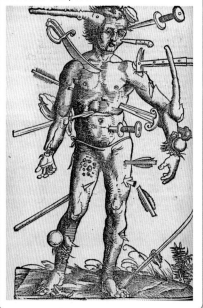

Think questions direct you to the things you should be noticing or thinking about in the sources and text. They also help you practise the kind of analytical skills that you need to improve in history.

THINK

You have probably studied nineteenth-century Britain before. You may be quite an expert already. So what do you think of our visual summary of this period? Discuss these questions.

1 Do you agree with the images we have chosen to summarise nineteenth-century Britain? What do you think we have left out?

2 Which images would you use to sum up life in Britain at this time? Why?

3 How much change do you think there was between 1800 and 1900?

KEY WORDS

Make sure you know what these words mean, and are able to use them confidently in your own writing. See the Glossary on pages 111–112 for definitions.
- Autopsy
- Cauterise
- Doctrine of signatures

Every subject and topic has its own vocabulary. If you don't know what these words mean you won't be able to write about the subject. So for each chapter we have provided a **key word** list. These are the kind of words or terms that could be used in sources or an exam question without any explanation, so you need to be able to understand them and use them confidently in your writing. They are all defined in the **Glossary** on pages 111–112. But we also want you to create your own key word list – in a notebook or on your phone, write down each word with your own definition.

TOPIC SUMMARY

Prevention of disease
- Edward Jenner discovered how to stop people catching smallpox.

Finally, there is a **Topic Summary** at the end of every topic. This condenses all the content into a few points, which should help you to get your bearings in even the most complicated content. You could read that summary before you even start the topic to know where you are heading!

b) It will help you to apply what you learn

The second big aim of this book is to help you apply what you learn, which means to help you think deeply about the content, develop your own judgements about the themes, and make sure you can support those judgements with evidence and relevant knowledge.

This is not an easy task. You will not suddenly develop this skill. You need to practise studying an issue, deciding what you think, and then selecting from all that you know the points that are really relevant to your argument. One of the most important skills in history is the ability to select, organise and deploy (use) knowledge to answer a particular question.

EARLY MODERN BRITAIN		
Factor	Relative importance of the factor	Positive or negative influence
War		
Superstition and religion		
Chance		
Government		
Communication		
Science and technology	5	+
The economy		
Ideas		
Role of the individual		

The main way we help you with this is through the **Focus Tasks**. These are the big tasks that appear at the end of each chapter so that you can build your big picture of the story of Health and the People. We ask you to create a:
- **What happened if you fell ill in …? chart** at the end of each period so you can track the way medicine, surgery and public health changed over time.
- **Factor card** noting examples of how different factors have caused change.

These tasks help you think through the big issues and the resulting charts will also help you revise.

Most Focus Tasks have tips that help you get started – highlighting a couple of key points that you can use in your answers.

c) It will help you prepare for your examination

If you read all the text and tackle all the Focus Tasks in this book you should be well prepared for the challenges of the exam, but to help you more specifically:

PROGRESS CHECK

Usefulness of sources
1 How useful is Source 1 for finding out about medieval medicine?

Significance
2 Who was the most significant in the development of medieval medicine, Hippocrates or Galen?

Progress Check questions focus on the skills and concepts that will be the focus of exam questions. These are not exam-style questions – but they deal with the kind of issues that the exams will focus on (usefulness of sources, significance of events, causes of events, factors for change, similarities and differences between events). They help you judge how well your thinking is developing about these issues.

Assessment Focus appears on pages 106–108. These pages take you step by step through the requirements of the specification and the kinds of questions you might be asked. They provide some **practice questions** and some sample answers that help you to see what an effective answer might look like.

Introduction: The big story of health and the people

FOCUS

A thematic unit covers a vast period of time – over 1,000 years – and includes a lot of detail. Each chapter covers the continuing story of the development of medicine and public health in Britain. But you will need to keep on connecting these little stories to the big story. That is what this introduction helps you with. It gives you an overview of the themes you will be studying and some activities to help you see the patterns over time. Good luck!

Feeling poorly

What happens today when you feel unwell? Where do you go to get help? Perhaps you self-diagnose. You go either to the supermarket or the pharmacy and buy medicine, or perhaps ask the pharmacist's advice. How do you know the medicine you buy is safe to use? How do you know it will work? You've probably seen adverts on the television or in the newspaper, but how do you really know it is safe to take and to use? Who controls the development and marketing of medicines today? Who do you think did in medieval times? Did they even have medicine in medieval times?

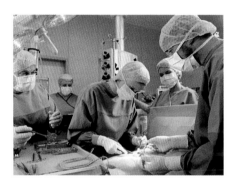

You might visit an 'alternative medicine' provider. Some people prefer 'natural healing', using herbs and traditional methods, such as Chinese acupuncture, homeopathy or osteopathy. More and more people are convinced that the best way to diagnose illness and then cure it is through natural remedies.

If it is an emergency you might go straight to the Accident and Emergency department of your local hospital, or call an ambulance to take you there. You might have a bit of a wait but there is emergency treatment available 24/7, with nursing staff and hospital consultants on call to deal with all kinds of emergencies.

Most likely you will make an appointment with your GP. It is usually possible to get an appointment within a day or so. Once there you might see the doctor, a nurse-practitioner or even the practice nurse. Whoever you see will try to decide what is wrong with you using a variety of techniques. They might take your temperature: when was the thermometer invented? How did they take your temperature before thermometers? They might listen to your breathing using a stethoscope. How did they do that before stethoscopes were invented? They might ask for a urine sample: this is widely used to test for some illnesses. Or they might take a blood test. Perhaps they might just look at you, or listen to what you have to say. If they can decide what is wrong with you they might issue a prescription for medicine and send you on your way.

But what if they can't decide? What happens then? In all probability you will be referred to a specialist, and have yet more tests. Eye tests, MRI scans, physio tests; specialists have a huge array of tests to probe and try to discover the cause of your ill-health. It might be a quick process, but sometimes it takes a long time to finally discover the *cause* of your illness.

Thinking about Health and the People

ACTIVITY

Below you can see some of the events that help us to tell the story of Health and the People over the last 3,000 years or so. Can you put these events in the appropriate place on the timeline?

1 Draw your own version of the timeline below and pencil in each of the events in the appropriate place.
2 You will find the correct dates for each of these events at the bottom of page 4. Plot the correct dates onto your timeline.
3 Which of these answers do you find surprising?
4 What does your timeline tell us about Health and the People?

You will be coming back to this timeline after you have finished the topic and will then have the opportunity to amend your thinking.

Event A: Treatments – penicillin, the first antibiotic

'We had an enormous number of wounded with infections, terrible burn cases among the crews of armoured cars. The usual medicines had absolutely no effect. The last thing I tried was penicillin. The first man was a young man called Newton. He had been in bed for six months with fractures of both legs. His sheets were soaked with pus. Normally he would have died in a short time. I gave three injections of penicillin a day and studied the effects under a microscope. The thing seemed like a miracle. In ten days' time the leg was cured and in a month's time the young fellow was back on his feet. I had enough penicillin for ten cases. Nine were complete cures.'

Event B: Treatments – herbal medicine

'Medicine for dimness of the eyes: take the juice of the celandine plant, mix with bumblebees' honey, put in a brass container then warm until it is cooked and apply to the eyes.'

Event C: Explaining disease – the Four Humours

Hippocrates wrote: 'Man's body contains Four Humours – blood, phlegm, yellow bile and melancholy (black) bile. When all these humours are truly balanced, he feels the most perfect health. Illness occurs when there is too much or too little of one of these humours or one is entirely thrown out of the body.'

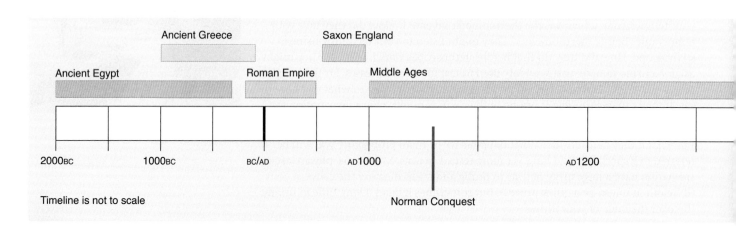

Timeline is not to scale

Event D: Explaining disease – God sends disease

'Terrible is God towards men. He sends plagues of disease and uses them to terrify and torment men and drive out their sins. That is why the realm of England is struck by plagues – because of the sins of the people.'

Event F: Explaining disease – Pasteur and germ theory

Louis Pasteur, a French scientist, published his 'germ theory' suggesting that bacteria or 'germs' were the true causes of diseases. His germ theory replaced all previous ideas about the causes of disease.

Event H: Treatments – wash, exercise, diet

'Every day wash face and eyes with the purest water and clean the teeth using fine peppermint powder. Begin the day with a walk. Long walks between meals clear out the body, prepare it for receiving food and give it more power for digesting.'

Event J: Public health – fresh water, baths and sewers

Sextus Julius Frontinus wrote: 'There was a great increase in the number of reservoirs, fountains and water-basins. As a result the air is purer. Water is now carried through the city to LATRINES, baths and houses.'

Event E: Public health – the NHS begins

'On the first day of free treatment on the NHS, Mother went and got tested for new glasses. Then she went further down the road to the chiropodist and had her feet done. Then she went back to the doctor's because she'd been having trouble with her ears and the doctor said he would fix her up with a hearing aid.'

Event G: Treatments – the black cat remedy

'The stye on my right eyelid was still swollen and inflamed very much. It is commonly said that rubbing the eyelid with the tail of a black cat will do it much good so, having a black cat, a little before dinner I tried it and very soon after dinner the swelling on my eyelid was much reduced and almost free of pain.'

Event I: Surgery – without anaesthetics

Robert Liston, a famous London surgeon, once amputated a man's leg in two and a half minutes but worked so fast he accidentally cut off his patient's testicles as well. During another high-speed operation Liston amputated the fingers of his assistant and slashed the coat of a spectator who, fearing he had been stabbed, dropped dead with fright. Both the assistant and the patient then died of infection caught during the operation or on the hospital ward. Liston worked really fast because there were no ANAESTHETICS.

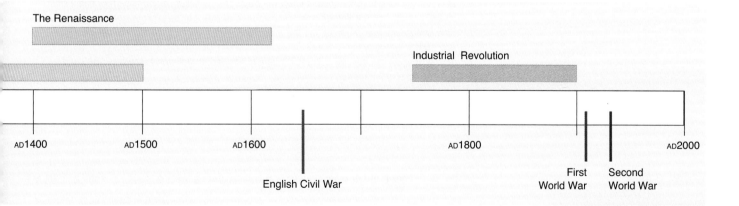

The Renaissance

Industrial Revolution

AD1400   AD1500   AD1600   AD1800   AD2000

English Civil War

First World War

Second World War

Treating the sick

Deciding what is wrong with you is only half the battle. How do you put it right? What *cure* should the doctor use to put right any illness? There are plenty of potential cures to choose from. Whole industries have grown up producing medicines, tablets and technology to treat patients, and to make money out of it. How is the doctor or specialist to decide which is the best treatment to use? What works for one person might not work for another. And how do they decide the right level of dose in each particular case? In other words, how do they get the 'cure' right?

Feeling poorly in the seventeenth century

In early 1685 King Charles II felt poorly. He called in his doctors. According to some accounts there were fourteen of them, who were often arguing over cause and potential cure. They were, of course, supposed to be the best doctors in the country! On 2 February Charles fainted, so the doctors had to decide what to do. First, they bled him, taking over 400ml of blood from his right arm. He did not respond, so they took another 200ml of blood, and gave him an EMETIC, to make him vomit. This was a mixture of antimony, sacred bitters, rock salt, mallow leaves, violet, beet root, camomile flowers, fennel seed, linseed, cinnamon, cardamom seed, saffron, cochineal and aloes. This would, in theory, clear any impurities out of his system. The next day they took more blood (300ml this time), and gave him a mixture of barley water and syrup to gargle. He was also given more laxatives to clear out his bowels. His treatment seemed to consist of continuous blood-letting, laxatives and emetics. Not surprisingly he became weaker and weaker. He didn't respond to the treatments and on the morning of 6 February Charles II died.

Recent research suggests that King Charles II died of kidney failure, probably linked to gout. Gout was a common disease among the upper classes at the time. The very worst treatment for kidney failure is to bleed a patient, so it appears that King Charles' doctors played a large part in killing him! So why did they bleed him? What were they trying to do? Were doctors in the seventeenth century so ignorant that they did not know the cause of the illnesses they were being asked to treat? Is the situation any different today? Today's doctors still find it hard to pinpoint the cause of some illnesses, and to effectively treat them.

Medicine mini-dictionary

As you work your way through this book you will come across various herbs, medicines, diseases or operations that you may not have heard of before. When you do, carry out your own research to find out about them. Write your own definition of each one, with notes, and create your own mini-dictionary of medicine through time.

THINK

1   Do you think King Charles' doctors knew the *cause* of his illness? Do you think they had a clear idea of how to *cure* the illness?
2   How similar, and how different, are the ways that Charles' doctors and modern-day doctors approach someone who is unwell?
3   In your opinion, has the way sickness is treated improved, or got worse, between 1685 and today? Explain your answer.

But people are healthier now, right?

You would think that people are healthier in today's world. People eat better, more regular meals, have higher incomes, there is much more food available, the majority are well-housed and warm, people are educated into making healthy choices. Surely that means they are healthier today? But it seems not everyone agrees.

Human Teeth Healthier in the Stone Age Than Today

(*Health Magazine*, 19 February 2013)

Medieval diets were far more healthy. If they managed to survive plague and pestilence, medieval humans may have enjoyed healthier lifestyles than their descendants today.

(BBC News website, 18 December 2007)

The UK is among the worst in western Europe for levels of overweight and obese people. In the UK, 67% of men and 57% of women are either overweight or obese. More than a quarter of children are also overweight or obese – 26% of boys and 29% of girls.

(*Guardian*, 29 May 2014)

The stories above cast doubt on the idea of people being healthier today than ever before. The story from *Health Magazine* is based on archaeological examination of teeth. They found evidence of fewer cavities, less oral disease and bone disorder than today. The BBC News website story is based on research into medieval records carried out by a Shropshire GP. The *Guardian* news story is taken from NHS England statistics. Can it really be the case that people today are less healthy than in medieval times? How can we investigate this idea further? How might you measure if people are healthier now than in previous periods of history?

One measure might be how long people live – if people live longer today then surely that means they are healthier?

THINK

4 What are the strengths of figures such as those showing the average age of death?

5 What are the limitations of these kinds of figures? Remember, even as late as 1900 INFANT MORTALITY was as high as 170 for every 1,000 live births, while today it is below 4. High infant mortality means that *average* figures for LIFE EXPECTANCY are lowered.

6 According to the data in Source 1, when were British men healthiest? How can you tell?

7 According to this data, when were British men unhealthiest? How can you tell?

8 How tall do you think, on average, British men will be in:
   a) 2100
   b) 2200
   c) 2500?

SOURCE 1

Average height of British males, compiled from various sources, but mostly skeletal data

Period	Average male height
Anglo-Saxons	5ft 6"
Normans	5ft 8"
Medieval	5ft 8"
Seventeenth century	5ft 5"
Victorians	5ft 5"
Twentieth century	5ft 8"
Today	5ft 10"

Died aged 40 — Anglo-Saxon
Died aged 35 — Medieval
Died aged 36 — Seventeenth century
Died aged 46 — Victorians
Died aged 60 — 1930s
Died aged 65 — 1950s
Died aged 80 — Today

Average age of death, of British males, compiled from various sources

The evidence is pretty clear from the data above. Men, on average, now live twice as long as they did in Anglo-Saxon times. Surely that tells us that men, at least, are healthier today than 1,000 years ago? But will our ideas change if we use another set of statistical data?

THINK

9 Can you think of any other measures we might use to decide whether or not people are healthier today than in previous centuries?

Making sense of all this data

SOURCE 2

A healthy living pyramid showing the proportions of different food groups in a healthy diet

People are living longer, and growing taller, at least according to the data shown here. Does that mean we are healthier? The figures on the previous page refer solely to men, and are averages. These figures therefore are only part of the picture. (There is much less skeletal data for women, for example, hence there is not enough reliable information to compile a 'height' list for women covering the period we are studying.) Leaving aside the limitations of the data we are faced with a series of conflicting evidence; some data suggest people are now healthier, but equally some suggest people may live longer but are not necessarily healthier. How can we reconcile this conundrum, and begin to reach a conclusion?

It is very easy to get data for today, and for the last two centuries. Since Victorian times government has collected masses of data about every aspect of people's lives. But how do you find meaningful data from the seventeenth century, or the thirteenth century? Would it perhaps be more helpful if we looked at child mortality, or deaths in childbirth: both of which have been major killers throughout much of history? What other aspects of people's lives might we consider?

Nowadays people are bombarded with advice on how to live a more healthy life: drink less alcohol, give up smoking, take more exercise, eat less sugar and fats, and so on. Nearly every week it seems new advice appears to help people deal with their unhealthy lifestyle choices. New diets are continually proposed. One of the latest is the 'Stone Age diet', where you eat and exercise like Stone-Age hunter-gatherers.

THINK

1 Find out what you would eat if you were to follow the Stone Age diet.
2 Why, if people are healthier than ever before, do they need all this advice?
3 Why are modern people so obese?
4 What are the foods we eat that are bad for us? And who decides?

ACTIVITY

1 On your own version of the table below, keep your own 'food diary' for a week. Make a note of what you eat and when.

	Monday	Tuesday	Wednesday	Thursday	Friday	Saturday	Sunday
Breakfast food							
Breakfast drinks							
Lunch food							
Lunch drinks							
Dinner food							
Dinner drinks							
Snacks							

2 Study the 'healthy living pyramid' in Source 2. Then, using a different colour to represent each section of the pyramid, highlight your food diary to show how much food you are eating from each of the different groups.

3 Now use the pyramid to decide whether or not you are eating healthily.

4 If you are eating unhealthily, make a list of ways in which you could change your diet to make it healthier.

Keeping clean

You have already discovered from your timeline activity (see page 2) that the Ancient Greeks clearly knew of the link between cleanliness and healthiness. So why was it so difficult to keep clean throughout most of history?

The answer is much the same as the reason most people drank ale or 'small beer' instead of water throughout most of history – not because they were addicted to alcohol but because water was both expensive and very dirty! It was quite common for waste to be discharged into a river before drinking water was taken out of the same river. There were few laws and health regulations. Local corporations (councils) and mayors were reluctant to take action to provide clean water because it would cost money, and, as most people were relatively poor, it would be the small number of richer people who would have to foot the bill. People had to collect their water from wherever they could. That often meant the local river or stream. What is surprising is the lengths people went to in order to try to keep themselves and their houses clean. Some towns had public baths from the early 1500s and, of course, if you were rich you could have your own private water supply brought direct to your house.

SOURCE 3

A twentieth-century impression of life in medieval London

THINK

5 Why was it so difficult for most people to keep clean throughout most of history?
6 Do you agree that people are healthier today than they were in other periods of history?

Organising your thinking

At the end of each chapter you will be completing a 'What happened to you if you fell ill?' table. This consists of five different columns shown here, designed to help you reflect on the content you have studied in each chapter. Here we outline how this table works.

Diseases

Rich or poor/ Town or country/ Old or young

Practitioners

Likely treatment	Likely outcome

Everyone today gets treated the same, don't they?

If you are ill then under the National Health Service everyone has equal access to care, at least in theory. Whether you are rich or poor, live in the town or the countryside, are young or old, you get treated by the NHS. But consider this newspaper story, from January 2015, highlighting the inequalities in cancer care. It reports that in deprived areas patients sometimes get poorer treatment than in richer areas.

> **National Audit Report highlights gap between rich and poor which could prevent 20,000 deaths per year**
>
> (*Daily Mirror*, 15 January 2015)

Was this the case in the past? Did everyone get the appropriate treatment whether they could pay for it or not? We have already seen that King Charles II was treated very differently to any patient today, and he presumably had plenty of money to pay for medical attention.

Which kind of medical professional would you be treated by?

We have already seen that today you might be treated by a GP, a nurse-practitioner, a nurse, a specialist, a pharmacist or even someone who uses alternative medicine, depending upon your choice and circumstances. Some professionals you can approach directly, others you have to be referred to. There is a huge range of specialists highly trained in one area of expertise to ensure you get the best possible treatment. But was that always the case in the past?

What kind of treatment might you receive?

Again, there is a huge choice of treatments available, both to NHS and PRIVATE PATIENTS. Sometimes the patient is offered a choice of treatments, or even the opportunity to decline treatment if they so wish. Science and technology today play a huge part in both diagnosis (deciding what is wrong with you) and treatment. Again, we have already seen the difference in how Charles II was treated in the 1600s and how he would have been treated today. Was treatment even more different in medieval times, before the Renaissance and the beginnings of scientific enquiry?

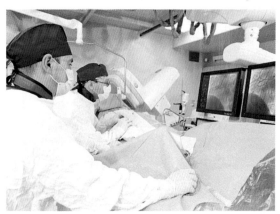

How successful might your treatment be?

Most doctors today would be very surprised if their 'cures' for various illnesses didn't work. It might take a while to find the correct dose, or the right medicine, but usually, in most cases, patients recover. Some illnesses are more deadly than others. Some cancer recovery rates are still very low, for example. But other illnesses that were fatal in times gone by, like measles, have all but been eradicated.

Why things change

For each chapter you will create a factor chart, like the one below, to identify the most important factors for change. Examples throughout the period are shown here. We need also to consider *why* changes occur, and the consequences of these changes.

SOURCE 4

Killer diseases of late twentieth-century Britain (Source: Office of National Statistics)

Cancer
Heart disease
Respiratory disease (e.g. flu)
Liver disease
Dementia/Alzheimer's disease
Accidents

THINK

Study Source 4.

1 Which of these diseases do you think of as 'old people's' diseases?
2 Which of these diseases do you think of as 'young people's' diseases?
3 Which do you think of as 'lifestyle' or 'affluence' diseases?
4 Which do you think were killer diseases in earlier times?

ACTIVITY

1 Can you think of one more example from history where each of these factors has created change?
2 Share these with the rest of your group and make a list for the classroom wall.

Factor	How each factor might influence health
War	The improvement of hygiene in hospitals because of the Crimean War
Superstition and religion	The setting up of medical schools and universities in medieval times in order to better train physicians
Chance	Alexander Fleming's discovery of penicillin
Government	The Labour Government introduces the NHS
Communication	William Caxton develops the printing press
Science and technology	The development of the microscope, probably in the Netherlands, in the 1590s
The economy	Pensions, introduced in 1909, because the economy was doing so well the rich could pay more tax
Ideas	The Beveridge Report in 1942 changed ideas by talking about the 'Five Great Evils'. This led to the Labour Party adopting the idea of a NHS, which they introduced when they won the 1945 election
Role of the individual	Edward Jenner pushes through his ideas on vaccination for smallpox

Medicine stands still

1

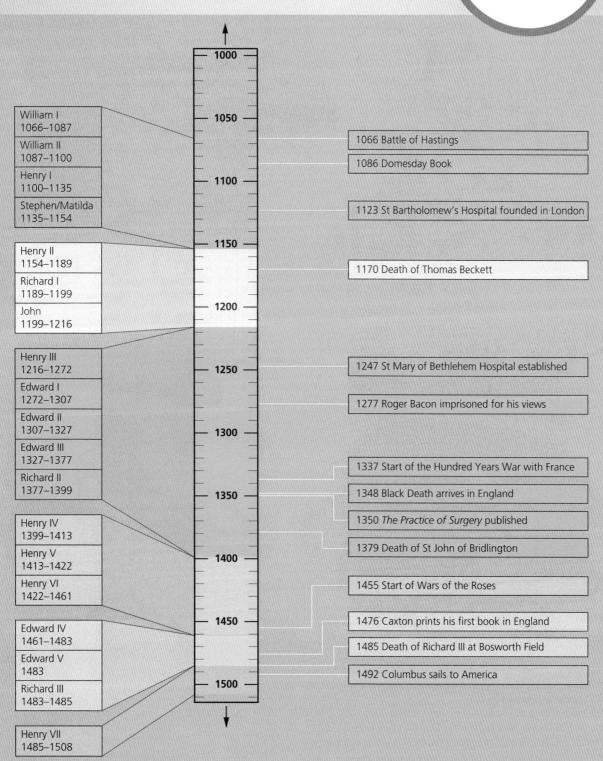

Monarchs	Timeline	Events
William I 1066–1087	1000	
William II 1087–1100	1050	1066 Battle of Hastings
Henry I 1100–1135	1100	1086 Domesday Book
Stephen/Matilda 1135–1154		1123 St Bartholomew's Hospital founded in London
Henry II 1154–1189	1150	1170 Death of Thomas Beckett
Richard I 1189–1199	1200	
John 1199–1216		
Henry III 1216–1272	1250	1247 St Mary of Bethlehem Hospital established
Edward I 1272–1307		1277 Roger Bacon imprisoned for his views
Edward II 1307–1327	1300	
Edward III 1327–1377		1337 Start of the Hundred Years War with France
Richard II 1377–1399	1350	1348 Black Death arrives in England
		1350 *The Practice of Surgery* published
Henry IV 1399–1413		1379 Death of St John of Bridlington
Henry V 1413–1422	1400	1455 Start of Wars of the Roses
Henry VI 1422–1461	1450	1476 Caxton prints his first book in England
Edward IV 1461–1483		1485 Death of Richard III at Bosworth Field
Edward V 1483		1492 Columbus sails to America
Richard III 1483–1485	1500	
Henry VII 1485–1508		

1.1 Context: Medieval Britain

THINK

1 How would *you* summarise life in medieval Britain? Do you agree with the images we have chosen, or not? What do you think we have left out? Which images would you use to sum up life in medieval Britain? Why?
2 How much change do you think there was between 1066 and the 1450s?
3 Do you think people were better off in 1450 than they were in 1066?
4 What do you think happened to you if you fell ill in a medieval village?

Being ill in medieval times

Life for many people in medieval times was nasty, hard and short, but how long you lived, and your chances of surviving illness depended as much on who you were as on what treatment you received – if any! The rich were more likely to be able to afford treatment by a doctor than the poor, and you were more likely to find a medical practitioner in a town than elsewhere. Towns were more deadly places to live than villages, the young were more at risk than adults, and winter brought its own special problems. But then again, so did summer!

Medieval diseases

Famine and war were perhaps the main killers of this period. A bad harvest due to drought or flood, too hot or too cold weather, meant MALNOURISHMENT for many, and malnourished people more easily catch disease. 'Saint Anthony's disease' was caused by a fungus growing on stored rye in damp conditions. Once the rye was ground into flour and baked into bread, those who ate it developed painful rashes and in some cases, even died. Dysentery, typhoid, smallpox and measles were all widespread. Some historians estimate that perhaps 10 per cent of England's population in the early fourteenth century died of these diseases. Childbirth was a dangerous time for women, and it is also likely that 30 per cent of children died before the age of seven.

Accidents were common too:

> At Aston, Warwickshire in October 1387, Richard Dousyng fell when a branch of the tree he had climbed broke. He landed on the ground, breaking his back, and died shortly after.

Not surprisingly, medieval people didn't really understand the causes of most diseases so they focused on trying to cure the symptoms instead. The best practitioners tried, following Hippocrates, to do no harm to their patients. But many of the treatments seem brutal and harmful to us. For example, a common 'remedy' for rheumatism was to wear a donkey skin and a treatment for asthma involved swallowing some young frogs. Perhaps you might prefer the treatment for ringworm – wash your hair daily with a male's urine!

Not all cures were so fanciful, however. *Bald's Leechbook*, a tenth-century Anglo-Saxon medical text, suggests this cure for eye problems:

> Take cropleek and garlic, of both equal quantities, pound them well together, take wine and bullocks' gall, of both equal quantities, mix with the leek, put this then into a brazen vessel, let it stand nine days in the brass vessel, wring out through a cloth and clear it well, put it into a horn, and about night time apply it with a feather to the eye.

Modern microbiologists recently recreated this medicine and in tests found it to be at least as effective as modern medicines used to treat the superbug MRSA. Perhaps those old herbalists really did know a thing or two about how to treat disease…

SOURCE 1

Vomiting a fox, from an illuminated manuscript

THINK

5   Study Source 1. Do you think medieval people really vomited a fox? If not, why is this picture included in a medieval manuscript? What does it tell us about our sources for medieval medicine?

6   Why do you think young people were so at risk of dying from ill-health in medieval times?

7   Which of the medieval killer diseases are still dangerous today?

8   Can you explain why a medicine from *Bald's Leechbook* in the tenth century should be as effective as a modern medicine? What does that tell us about medieval medicine?

a) A Stone Age skull trepanned   b) An Indus Valley sewer

c) An ancient Egyptian physician   d) A Greek Asclepion

e) A Roman aqueduct   f) A Muslim doctor treating his patient

1.2 Where did medieval ideas about health come from?

FOCUS

Archaeological evidence has revealed that successful medical care was taking place as far back as the Stone Age. Civilisations like Ancient Egypt, Ancient Greece and Ancient Rome had hospitals, medical experts and texts widely available, and were in fact more advanced than in the West. This topic explores these methods and beliefs, and focuses particularly on the pioneering and influential work of Hippocrates and Galen.

Look at the illustrations on the left. People have always known how to look after themselves. There is clear evidence of successful operations carried out with flint tools in the Stone Age. Archaeological evidence shows that some of these patients survived. The Indus Valley civilisation was well aware of the importance of clean running water and sewers. There is even a structure identified as a huge public bath-house in Mohen Daro in Pakistan, dating from around 2500BC. Pharaohs in Ancient Egypt had their court physicians, and we know about some of their medical practices from papyrus records recovered from tombs. The Greeks had ASCLEPIONS, or places of healing, that were temples to Asclepius, the god of healing. The Romans went to great lengths to bring fresh water to their towns and cities. Bath-houses and underfloor heating can be found in most Roman towns, for example Vindolanda in Northumberland. And, as we have already discovered, *Bald's Leechbook* is an Anglo-Saxon medical text full of remedies and medicines.

The influence of Arab medicine

Yet much of this medical knowledge seems to have been 'lost' during the so-called 'Dark Ages', after the Romans left. Muslim writers like Avi Senna played a very important role in saving much of this lost knowledge, translating the works of Ancient Greece and Rome into Arabic, which was eventually passed on to western Europe. At this time there is no doubt that Arabic medicine was much in advance of that in western Europe (see Source 1). Avicenna was one of the most celebrated philosophers and physicians in the early Islamic Empire. He wrote many texts on a wide range of subjects. Forty of his medical texts have survived, the most famous of which are the *Kitab ash-Shifa* (the *Book of Healing*) and the *al-Qanun fi al-Tibb* (*Canon of Medicine*). The latter is one of the most significant books in the history of medicine; for instance, it was printed in Europe at least 60 times between 1516 and 1574. The *Canon* remained a major authority for medical students in both the Islamic world and Europe until well into the 1700s. Another Arab doctor, Rhazes, who lived from AD860 to 932, wrote the first authentic description of the symptoms of smallpox.

From their establishment in the AD900s, Islamic hospitals were sites of medical education as well as healing. The most famous hospitals, including those in Baghdad, Damascus and Cairo, contained lecture rooms, pharmacies and libraries. As important as reading and mastering texts in the Islamic tradition was instruction – many students received practical training in hospitals. Some even observed patients at the bedside. Cleanliness was encouraged and hospitals were often centred around fountains, and cooling breezes circulated around the wards.

SOURCE 1

Muslim doctor Usama ibn Munqidh writing in around 1175

They brought to me a knight with a sore on his leg; and a woman who was feeble-minded. To the knight I applied a small POULTICE; and the woman I put on a diet to turn her humour wet. Then a French doctor came and said, 'This man knows nothing about treating them'. He then said, 'Bring me a sharp axe'. Then the doctor laid the leg of the knight on a block of wood and told a man to cut off the leg with the axe, upon which the marrow flowed out and the patient died on the spot. He then examined the woman and said, 'There is a devil in her head'. He therefore took a razor, made a deep cross-shaped cut on her head, peeled away the skin until the bone of the skull was exposed, and rubbed it with salt. The woman also died instantly.

THINK

1   What, according to Usama ibn Munqidh (Source 1), were the main differences between Muslim and European medicine?
2   Can you explain these differences?

Hippocrates and Galen

Two men, perhaps more than any others, contributed to the Western view of medicine and health at this time. They were Hippocrates and Galen.

The theory of the Four Humours

Hippocrates wrote:

'The human body contains blood, phlegm, yellow bile and black bile. These are the things that make up its constitution and cause its pains and health. Health is primarily that state in which these constituent substances are in the correct proportion to each other, both in strength and quantity, and are well mixed. Pain occurs when one of the substances presents either a deficiency or an excess, or is separated in the body and not mixed with others.'

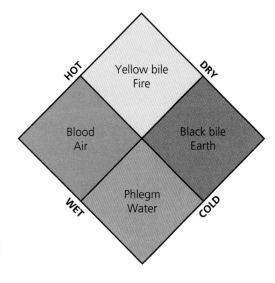

So to remain healthy a body needed to keep the Four Humours in balance. As you can see from the diagram, some humours are 'hot' and therefore create sweating illnesses; and some humours are 'cold', creating illnesses such as melancholia. Different foods and different seasons could affect the humours, so it was important to do all things in moderation to keep the body in balance. Diagnosis was obviously very difficult and thus best left to the specialist!

The influence of Hippocrates and Galen

Galen's work arrived in Europe via Islamic texts and beliefs. Greek translations were made in Salerno, in Italy (the first medical university dating from around AD900), and rapidly became accepted as university medical texts. Church leaders looked carefully at Galen's works and decided that they fitted with Christian ideas because throughout he referred to 'the Creator'. Doctors believed his ideas were correct and that it was nearly impossible to improve his work. As Salerno was a common stopping-off point en route to the Holy Land, Galen's ideas rapidly spread throughout Europe and became accepted as medical orthodoxy. Even dissection was taught from Galen's book while an assistant would point to the relevant part of the body – and remember Galen was only allowed to dissect animals!

TOPIC SUMMARY

Where did medieval ideas about health come from?
- There is evidence of some effective medical care in Britain before medieval times.
- Medieval people placed great emphasis on the works of Hippocrates and Galen.
- Muslim medical care seemed to be much in advance of that in the West.
- Most medical theories were focused on the idea of balancing the Four Humours.

Hippocrates, 460–370BC
- Born in Kos, Greece, in 460BC.
- The first physician to regard the body as a whole, to be treated as a whole, rather than individual parts.
- Based his thinking around the Four Humours. These were to be kept in balance if a person was to be healthy.
- He believed in the importance of observation.
- Around 60 texts are attributed to Hippocrates, although many may have been written by his followers.
- He believed that diet and rest were hugely important for a patient's recovery.
- Regarded by many as the father of modern medicine.
- Even today, new doctors around the world still take the HIPPOCRATIC OATH.

Galen, AD130–c210
- Born in what is now Turkey, in AD130.
- Studied medicine in Egypt before moving to Rome.
- Took Hippocrates' ideas further.
- He practised the dissection of animals in order to better understand the human body.
- He worked for three years as a doctor in a gladiator school where his knowledge and techniques developed.
- He used the theory of the Four Humours, and emphasised the importance of listening to a patient's pulse.
- His ideas profoundly influenced Western ideas of medicine for a very long time.

PROGRESS CHECK

Usefulness of sources
1 How useful is Source 1 for finding out about medieval medicine?

Significance
2 Who was more significant in the development of medieval medicine, Hippocrates or Galen?

1.3 Medieval medicine

FOCUS

Medieval people had varying ideas of the causes of illness, and as physicians became more qualified, varying treatments were available. This topic will explore the different factors which decided how and by whom people were treated, and how the process of diagnosis was carried out.

What did medieval people think made them ill?

ACTIVITY

How well-trained were medieval medical practitioners?

As you work through this unit, make a note in a table, like this one, of each type of practitioner you come across, and how they were trained for their job. The first one has been done for you. You will return to your table at the end of this topic.

Medical practitioner	How they were trained
Arab doctor	Reading texts and working in a hospital

During this period people had a wide range of beliefs about the causes of illness.

God

Religion played a huge part in most people's lives so it is not surprising that people thought God had a part to play in the spread of disease. If someone was living a sinful life, then a difficult illness was God's way of punishing them for their sins. If society as a whole was being sinful, or moving away from the true path of faith and the directions of the Pope, then an EPIDEMIC or plague was a just reward, sent by God, to remind people of their duties to the Church.

There was also a belief in the DOCTRINE OF SIGNATURES. God had created illness, but in his kindness he had also created the right herbs or plants with which to treat that illness. All you had to do was identify that plant. Lungwort, for example, was to be used for breathing problems, and eyebright for eye infections. Some plants were said to look like the part of the body they were to be used to treat. Saxifrage, for example, breaks up rocks as it grows so it must be perfect for treating kidney stones; alkanet has viper-shaped seeds so it is perfect to use to treat snake bites.

Bad smells

Some people began to notice the link between disease and bad air, or bad smells. MORTALITY was higher in the towns and cities than in the countryside. People lived closer together, alongside their animals and their filth. Travellers often said you could smell a town long before you could see it. So it is hardly surprising that many people thought disease was spread by bad smells infecting neighbours and friends.

Everyday life

Most people believed illness and early death were inevitable. So many children died before the age of seven that in many ways it seemed quite natural. Also childbirth was a very dangerous time for women, and it was expected that a man would need to remarry to provide his children with a new mother. Warfare and famine were frequent. Everyday life was an uncertain business!

The supernatural

Mystery and magic and the supernatural world were used by some to explain unexpected happenings. Witchcraft was feared and many believed the world was full of demons trying to cause trouble and death. Any sudden diseases or misfortunes could easily be blamed on the supernatural, especially as the Church painted a picture of a life where 'good' fought 'evil'.

The Four Humours

But by far the widest-held belief was that people were ill because their Four Humours were out of balance. Every doctor agreed with Hippocrates and Galen that illness was caused by the loss of equilibrium. Every doctor had a chart showing which illnesses were caused by which Humour that they would use alongside a zodiac chart (see Source 5, page 16) showing the best time to treat illnesses, plan an operation or even pick the herbs needed for medicine.

ACTIVITY

1 Which do you think are the best explanations of the causes of illness outlined on this page? Rank them in order along a line like this one:

Best explanation   Worst explanation

2 Repeat the activity, this time showing which explanations you think medieval people would find most convincing. Can you explain any differences?

Who would treat the sick in medieval times?

SEVERE SHORTAGE OF GPS COULD SEE TRADITIONAL FAMILY DOCTOR BECOME A THING OF THE PAST

Maureen Baker, of the Royal College of General Practitioners, said there was a 'severe shortage' of family doctors and more needed to be done to encourage people into the profession. It means the tradition of having a family doctor from cradle to grave could soon be a thing of the past.

(*Daily Express*, 9 June 2015)

Most people who had the money would go to a barber-surgeon, who would carry out minor operations, set broken bones or pull teeth (see Source 1). To become a barber-surgeon you would need to serve an apprenticeship before becoming qualified. These practitioners were mostly found in towns and cities, although some made a living travelling around the countryside or with visiting fairs.

SOURCE 2

'Lessons in Dissection' by Granger, 1493, in Venice

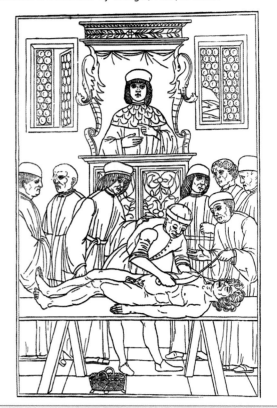

SOURCE 1

An image of medieval dentistry taken from a fourteenth-century encyclopedia

Ordinary people would almost certainly depend on the apothecary, who would sell medicines as well as herbs and spices from his shop in a town. He had probably served an apprenticeship for seven years with an existing apothecary to learn his trade. He would sell 'simples', a medicine made up of one plant or herb only; or 'compounds', which were a combination of ingredients made up to deal with a specific illness or complaint. One such compound was red rose, ground fine with bamboo juice, for treating smallpox. People might also visit the local 'wise woman'. She would have wisdom and skills handed down by her family that were probably as effective as anyone else's, she was reasonably priced and would usually know the patient already. Many of these women would also act as midwives, looking after women in labour. The 'lady of the house' would often be expected to provide medical care for the family, and, on an estate or farm, for labourers too. So there was medical care available in medieval times.

THINK

1 How did medical care differ between:
   a) rich and poor
   b) town and country?
2 Do you think medieval people were well-served by their medical personnel?
3 Would you have felt comfortable going to the doctor in medieval times?

SOURCE 3

Blood-letting in the late thirteenth century

SOURCE 4

A urine chart used by physicians in medieval times

SOURCE 5

A Greek zodiac chart from the fifteenth century

What treatments did medieval practitioners use?

How about this for a medieval headache remedy?

> Drink warm camomile tea and then lie down on rosemary and lavender-scented pillows for 15 minutes.

Or this one for aching joints?

> Take equal amounts of radish, bishopwort, garlic, wormwood, helenium, cropleek and hollowleek. Pound them up, and boil them in butter with celandine and red nettle. Keep the mixture in a brass pot until it is a dark red colour. Strain it through a cloth and smear on the forehead or aching joints.

Perhaps those apothecaries and wise women did know what they were doing! Some treatments were more fanciful, however. For toothache, which some people thought was caused by tooth worms burrowing into the tooth:

> Take a candle of sheep suet, some eringo (sea holly *Eryngium maritimum*) seed being mixed therewith, and burn it as near the tooth as possible, some cold water being held under the candle. The worms (destroying the tooth) will drop into the water, in order to escape from the heat of the candle.

The preferred way to fight illness, and restore the balance of the Four Humours, was by bleeding. This was done either by 'cupping' (see Source 3) or by using leeches. Monastery records show some monks were bled up to eight times a year! Illness was said to be caused by the body creating too much blood so it was obvious that bleeding a patient would restore their vitality. Interestingly, leeches are still used today in some hospitals to suck up blood and aid patient recovery!

Diagnosing illnesses

Doctors had two other indispensable tools for diagnosing sickness and putting it right: urine and the zodiac chart. Urine was a vital diagnostic tool. The physician would look carefully at the colour and compare it to a chart like the one shown in Source 4. He might smell it and, in some circumstances, taste it to help him decide what was wrong with the patient. Again, many patients today still have to submit a urine sample as part of the process of diagnosis.

Finally, no self-respecting physician would treat a patient without his most important tool – a zodiac chart like the one shown in Source 5. Charts like this would tell a physician which parts of the body were linked to which astrological sign, and thus dictate what the physician might do to cure a patient. For example, some things might work for an Aries (see the ram at the bottom of Source 5), but not for a Pisces (see the fish at the bottom of Source 5). The chart might also tell the physician the best time to carry out the treatment, and even when to pick the herbs used in medicines – herbs picked at the wrong time of the Moon's cycle, for example, might do more harm than good! It was a complicated business for physicians to decide what was causing an illness and how it might best be treated.

A case study: John Arderne – the first English surgeon?

John Arderne was born in Newark in 1307. He trained as a surgeon and practised in London. He became famous in his own lifetime for his astonishing success rate. In difficult operations removing growths from inside a patient's anus, he had a survival rate of over 50 per cent, which was quite astonishing for the fourteenth century!

We first discover John working for the Duke of Gaunt in the Hundred Years War. He was probably at the Battle of Crecy in 1346. His work as a surgeon on the battlefield helped him deal with major wounds. It was probably here too that he developed his own pain-killing ointment, made from hemlock, opium and henbane. This helped healing and stopped the need for CAUTERISING deep wounds, which had frequently led to the death of the patient. Being a war surgeon also helped him develop speedy amputation skills!

John went on to write books explaining his methods, which were widely read at the time. His most famous title was *The Practice of Surgery* written in 1350. In his works he advocated doctors having a good bedside manner, dressing soberly and talking to patients calmly and in a considered manner. He also urged doctors to trust their own judgement and experience and not rely on the old texts of Galen and Hippocrates. In fact, both his method of operating on fistulas (swellings inside the body) and his recommended bedside manner are very modern indeed. He charged the rich as much as he possibly could get away with for his services, as they could afford it, but he treated the poor for free.

THINK

1 Do you think John Arderne was a typical medieval surgeon?
2 How do *you* think he achieved a 50 per cent survival rate for surgery?

PROGRESS CHECK

Significance

1 How significant do you think John Arderne is in the story of medieval surgery?

Now answer this question:

2 Do you think that the title of this part of your course, 'Medicine stands still', is a good description of medicine at this time?

TOPIC SUMMARY

Medieval medicine

- People did not really understand the causes of illnesses at this time.
- Many different treatments were available if you could pay for them.
- Astrology was used to predict illnesses and suggest cures.
- Some people, like John Arderne, were beginning to take a more scientific approach to sickness.
- Many people did not have easy access to medical advice or treatment.

1.4 Medical progress

FOCUS

There was *some* progress in medicine at this time, both in diagnosing illness and in treating it. Some people were beginning to question Hippocrates and Galen, and as a number of autopsies took place, knowledge of the human body developed. This topic will assess the true extent of these developments, and the role of the first hospitals which had sprang up across the country.

What was the Church's role in medical progress in medieval times?

In medieval society the Church was central to most people's lives so its attitude to medicine had a profound influence on medical progress and developments. Most importantly, the Church encouraged people to pray for deliverance from illness, for forgiveness of their sins and to prepare for the after-life. (Remember, most surgery was extremely dangerous!) As well as prayer, offerings could buy INDULGENCES, and going on a pilgrimage to a holy shrine might bring about a cure. Pilgrims would often leave a miniature copy of the infected body part at the shrine, and hope that prayer and belief would bring about a cure.

SOURCE 1

A fifteenth-century stained-glass window depicting St John of Bridlington

St John of Bridlington

The most famous pilgrimage of course was to the HOLY LAND, but in England you could also visit Canterbury, Walsingham, Glastonbury or a host of other sites, like the Priory at Bridlington where St John of Bridlington's grave was a source of miracles – even Henry V went on pilgrimage there following his victory at Agincourt. John had been an Augustinian monk in Bridlington Priory all his life, eventually becoming prior there. He was renowned for his holiness and miracles were attributed to him while he was still alive. He was canonised (made a saint) in 1404, barely 30 years after his death. The site of his burial rapidly became a place of pilgrimage, especially for women in labour and sailors.

Helping progress

It was regarded as a central part of Christian duty to look after the poor and the sick, so the Church played a large part in developing hospitals and over 160 were set up in the twelfth and thirteenth centuries. Some of these were very small, many were attached to monasteries (see page 20) and some refused to take in very sick people or women, but there were at least some places for the sick to be treated.

The Church also set up university schools of medicine throughout Europe where physicians could be trained using the texts of Hippocrates and Galen. In fact, it was often through these university schools and in monasteries that the old texts were hand-copied by monks and thus survived, many of them arriving in the West in Arabic translations from the Islamic world.

Limiting progress

The Church also helped to limit medical progress. It made it very difficult for scholars to dissect human bodies, although there is evidence of autopsies taking place, like the one described in Source 2.

Most studies of dissection were still based on Galen's writings, but his work on dissection was based on working on animals. Therefore the Church's insistence on using Galen and his works widely, limited progress in understanding the workings of the human body. Scientists who tried to insist on scientific method and observation often ran into difficulty. Roger Bacon, a Franciscan monk and lecturer at Oxford University, was arrested around 1277 for spreading anti-Church views after questioning the Church's stance on Galen.

Other factors for progress

War was endemic in medieval times, and led to advances in surgery and the treatment of wounds. Cauterisation of wounds, applying great heat to the edges of the affected areas, was common, and designed to stop bleeding. It was extremely painful and, as often as not, fatal. This led some surgeons to use wine as an ANTISEPTIC to clean wounds, and others, such as John Arderne, to develop pain-relieving ointments to apply to wounds instead (see page 17). Opium began to be used as a painkiller. Draughts of the drug were designed to knock out patients to allow surgery to take place, but sometimes the opium- and hemlock-based liquids were too strong and killed the patient instead!

Army surgeons became very adept at quickly carrying out amputations with saw and knife, again a very painful business without effective anaesthetic. Finally new tools were developed, like the arrow cup, designed to slide into a deep wound, surround an arrow-head and gently remove it from the body without causing any more damage. Manuals helped to spread knowledge, and many would feature diagrams like the wound-man (Source 3), showing the kinds of wounds army surgeons could expect to treat during their career.

Science, too, played its part. Robert Grosseteste, teacher at the University of Oxford and then Bishop of Lincoln, was a leading advocate of scientific enquiry and experiment. His work on optics eventually led to the development of spectacles. Roger Bacon, as we have already seen, was imprisoned for challenging the Church's views on Galen and the importance of scientific method and close observation. People were beginning to question the old texts and the Church's insistence on agreeing with them.

ACTIVITY

1 Using the information on pages 18–19, make notes under the following three headings to show how each helped progress in medicine in medieval times:
   a) Church
   b) War
   c) Science
2 Which factor do you think helped progress in medicine the most?

SOURCE 2

A description of an autopsy in 1477

In August of 1477, Fiamatta di Donato Adimari gave birth to a daughter. Several weeks later she told her husband about an intense pain around her heart – two hours later she died. She was 25. Her husband, Filippo di Matteo Strozzi, a wealthy businessman, asked several physicians to perform an AUTOPSY. He later wrote: 'I had the body opened and among the others there to see it was Master Lodovico, a prominent Florentine physician, and he later said to me that he had found her uterus full of petrified [hardened] blood, and that this caused her death. And in addition, her liver was in very bad shape, together with her lungs, which had begun to attack her kidneys. So that if she had not died of this illness, she would have fallen into consumption.'

THINK

1 Why do you think the Church placed so much emphasis on prayer and pilgrimage as a way to cure illness?
2 In your opinion, overall, did the Church help or hinder medical progress in the medieval period?

SOURCE 3

A wound-man, 1517, designed to help army surgeons

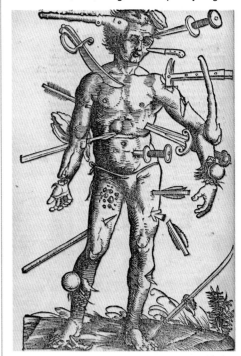

How safe were you in hospital?

Eadmer, a monk at Canterbury Cathedral, wrote this in the twelfth century, about Bishop Lanfranc's aim to establish and maintain a hospital:

> But I must not conclude my work by omitting what he did for the poor outside the walls of the city of Canterbury. In brief, he constructed a decent and ample house of stone … for different needs and conveniences. He divided the main building into two, appointing one part for men oppressed by various kinds of infirmities and the other for women in a bad state of health. He also made arrangements for their clothing and daily food, appointing ministers and guardians to take all measures so that nothing should be lacking for them.

But not everyone could be admitted to hospital:

> No lepers, no lunatics, no people with a contagious disease, no pregnant women, no sucking infants, no intolerable infants – even if they are poor and infirm, and if they are admitted by mistake, they are to be expelled. And when the other poor and infirm persons have recovered they are to be let out without delay.

(From the rules of the Hospital of St John, in Bridgewater, in 1215)

At least this last point suggested some people were expected to survive their illness and leave the hospital. They were not just envisaged as places to go to die.

So what were hospitals for? St Bartholomew's Hospital in London, set up in 1123, at first specialised in the treatment of poor, pregnant women. St Mary of Bethlehem, established in 1247, specialised in the treatment of 'poor and silly persons'. Many towns had leper houses outside their walls, or 'hospitality' places for travellers. Many small hospitals were, in effect, ALMSHOUSES set up to provide a home for the old and those unable to work, who might otherwise have had to live on the streets and beg for a living: not at all like a hospital today. Perhaps it is fair to say that early hospitals were in some ways the safe lodging houses of the medieval period. Many were funded by the Church, or by rich people leaving endowments to pay for a certain number of beds. Basically, they were care homes, where those in need could receive warmth, food and rest until they felt better.

Care within a hospital

The first thing that happened to you when you rang the doorbell in a medieval hospital was that you went to chapel. The next stop was the bath, and the nuns or sisters took your clothes, boiled them and baked them in the oven. You then went into clean sheets overnight. Very few hospitals employed either physicians or surgeons. Most care was carried out by nuns or elderly women – too old to tempt men into the ways of the flesh! The main treatment, however, was prayer. A priest would say mass every day, and the occupants would be expected to confess their sins and prepare to meet their God. Prayer and contemplation, in line with the Church's views on the cause of illness, were expected to bring about recovery. Most sisters, or monks if the hospital was attached to a monastery, would have plenty of knowledge of herbal remedies. In fact, excavations at Soutra, on the main road from Scotland to England, found an early Scottish establishment set up by Augustinian monks to be a hospital rather than a place of religion. It is the largest hospital discovered to date, and shows clear evidence of the use of quite sophisticated herbal remedies. Evidence found at the hospital site suggests the medieval Augustine monks knew how to amputate limbs, fashion surgical instruments, induce birth, stop scurvy and even create hangover cures. There was even evidence of them growing non-native herbs and plants to use in medical recipes.

SOURCE 4

Nurses tending to the sick, on a ward in the Hotel du Dieu, Paris

St Giles Hospital

St Giles Hospital in Norwich is a good example of a medieval hospital, set up by Bishop Walter de Suffield in 1249, and still in use today as a care home. It was named after St Giles, who was the patron saint of lepers, cripples and nursing mothers. It was established to care for the sick, but also for the remission of the bishop's sins so that when he died he would spend less time in PURGATORY and get into Heaven quicker! A priest was to say a prayer for his soul every day, and to make the patients pray for him too. The bishop set up the hospital on about ten acres of land in Norwich and funded it with the income from several churches around Norwich. Other local people – rich and not so rich – left money and land to the hospital to cover its running costs. There were strict rules as to who could and could not be admitted, and how they were to be looked after.

THINK

1 What was the main role of the first hospitals?
2 What were the motives of those setting up hospitals?
3 To what extent did hospitals reflect the Church's views on illness, medicine and health?

SOURCE 5

The grounds of St Giles Hospital in the early nineteenth century and some of the rules in force there

St Giles Hospital Rules

- There shall be a master to take good care of the hospital, and to work for the remission of Bishop Suffield's sins.
- There shall be at least three or four women, aged over fifty, who are to change the sheets and take care of the sick.
- Everyone must rise at the crack of dawn to say prayers.
- There will be a weekly mass in honour of St Giles.
- There will be thirty beds or more.
- There will be a poor box from which poor people passing by can receive alms and charitable assistance.
- The sisters are to sleep in a separate dormitory.
- No women are allowed to stay in the hospital as patients.

ACTIVITY

How well-trained were medieval medical practitioners?

Look back at the table that you started on page 14. You should now be in a position to answer this question about the training of medieval medical practitioners.

1 Use your table to draw up two lists: one giving examples of how well-trained people were; the other suggesting ways they were not well-trained.
2 What were the most important factors in limiting effective training?

TOPIC SUMMARY

Medical progress

- There was some progress in looking after sick people at this time.
- The Church believed prayer and pilgrimage were the best cure for illness.
- The Church played an important part in providing hospitals and monasteries to look after the old, the infirm and the sick.
- The establishment of the first hospitals saw the beginnings of treating people in specific settings.
- Herbal treatments still remained the usual form of medicine.
- The Church resisted some progression in medicine, such as the practice of autopsies.
- Texts, many arriving via the Arabic world, helped spread good practice among those prepared to listen to new ideas.

1.5 Public health in the Middle Ages

Medical moments in time: London, 1347

FOCUS

In the Middle Ages towns were much smaller, and fewer in number, than today, yet they were still very unhealthy places. Houses were crowded together and sanitation was very limited. This topic examines why this made them such unhealthy places to live, and how there were some attempts at hygiene in monasteries and some towns.

This pestilence is caused by stinking air so I will use an even more terrible smell to ward off the bad air carrying the pestilence. Twice a day I will put my head in a bucket full of PRIVY waste and breathe the fumes for half an hour. That will keep the pestilence away.

I treated arrow wounds with the King's army. A blacksmith made me a tool to take the arrow out. Then honey on the wound to help it heal. That'll teach you to walk behind the target at archery practice.

Some houses had toilets overhanging streams providing water for washing, cleaning and drinking.

Your humours are out of balance. Go to a surgeon who'll bleed you and go again in six months.

There were public toilets but one was over the Thames which supplied some of the city's water.

Wells for drinking water were often close to cesspools for dumping sewage.

A certain cure for the pestilence? A holy remedy made from the finest herb and dust from the true Holy Cross on which Christ was crucified. Only one silver penny!

ACTIVITY

Look carefully at this picture of London in 1347. Some of the things making life unhealthy are highlighted with a text box. Others are not. Make a list of all the unhealthy factors you can find.

Life in a town or city was fraught with danger. You might get killed by a cut-purse (pickpocket), trapped in a fire or run over by a horse and cart. Accidents while carrying out normal everyday chores were common, as the case of Johanna Appulton shows. In August 1389 she was drawing water when she fell into the well. The incident was witnessed by a servant who ran to her aid, and while helping her fell in as well. This was overheard by a third person who went to their aid – he too fell in, and all three subsequently drowned.

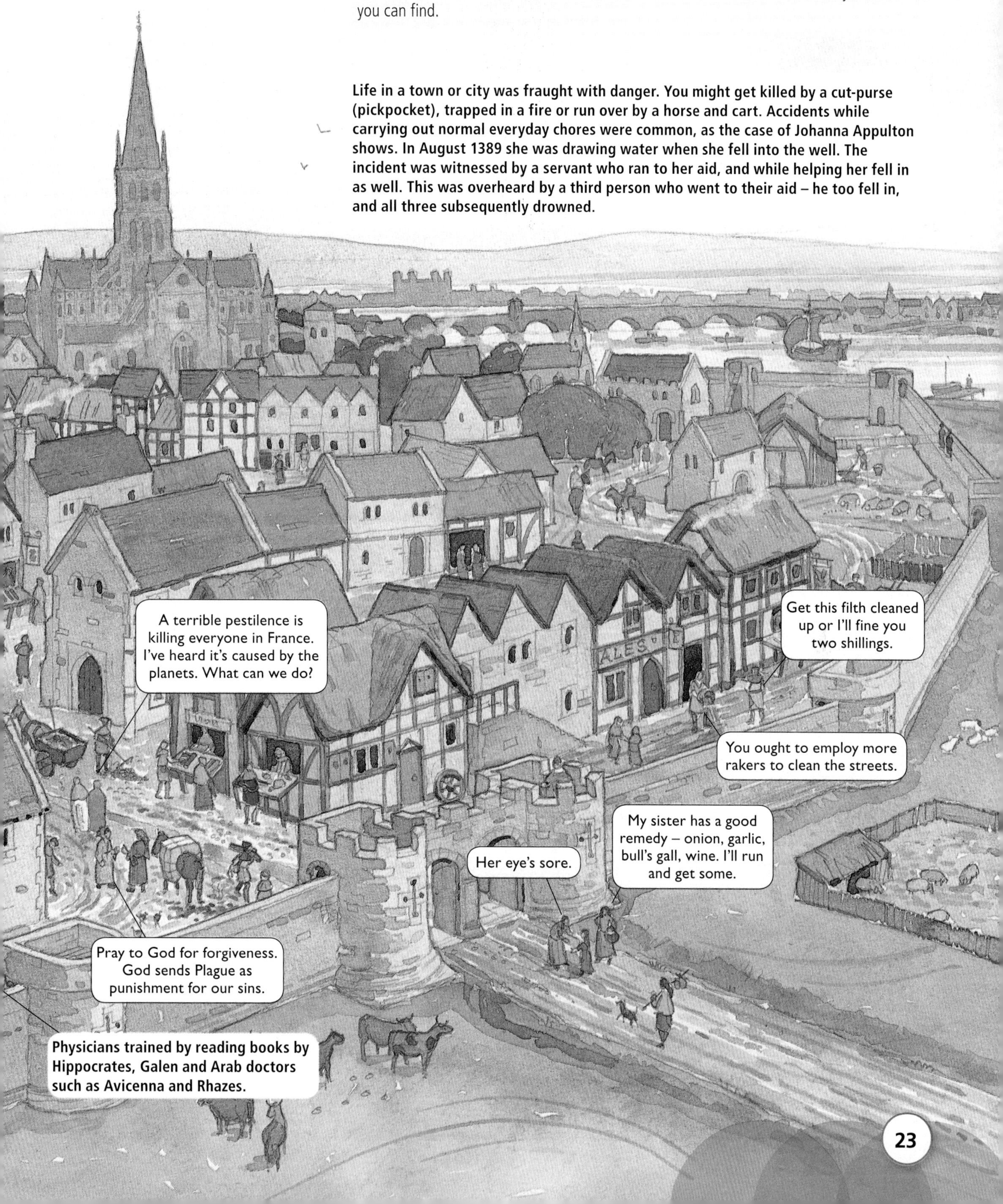

A terrible pestilence is killing everyone in France. I've heard it's caused by the planets. What can we do?

Get this filth cleaned up or I'll fine you two shillings.

You ought to employ more rakers to clean the streets.

My sister has a good remedy – onion, garlic, bull's gall, wine. I'll run and get some.

Her eye's sore.

Pray to God for forgiveness. God sends Plague as punishment for our sins.

Physicians trained by reading books by Hippocrates, Galen and Arab doctors such as Avicenna and Rhazes.

23

Why was living in towns and cities so unhealthy?

Towns were unhealthy because so many people lived so close together. There were few regulations about building or waste disposal. Clean water was in short supply, and water was often drawn from rivers and streams that were contaminated with waste. Butchers brought live animals into the town or city to slaughter them, leaving the problem of how to get rid of the waste. Industries like tanning (creating leather) were carried on nearby, creating smells and waste. There was no 'zoning' in towns so industry and houses were mixed together higgledy-piggledy. There were no dustbins or rubbish collectors to remove waste so it just accumulated in the streets until the rain washed it away. CESSPITS were often built next to wells, allowing the one to contaminate the other. Cesspits were also emptied infrequently as you had to pay people to remove the waste.

Everywhere there were animals: horses for transport, creating tons of dung every week; or domestic pigs roaming around eating scraps before being slaughtered. There were no sewers, so household waste was chucked out into the street and left to rot. If you were unlucky the overnight piss-pot might be chucked out of an upstairs window as you were passing below. Keeping food fresh was difficult, so you had to shop for food every day. Shopkeepers would try to sell food that was going off rather than throw it away. Water for washing, either clothes or people, was hard to come by, so people weren't overly clean. Water for drinking was also rare, hence most people would drink 'small beer' rather than risk the water. Conditions such as sewage in the streets in the countryside or small villages were not really a problem, but they became deadly in towns. Disease spread quickly. No wonder medical people thought disease was spread by bad smells!

SOURCE 1

A couple bathing, from an illuminated manuscript

How did monasteries help?

Monasteries knew of the dangers of dirt and filth. Most monasteries carefully extracted water for drinking, washing, cooking and brewing upstream of the privies, and then used the waste water to flush away the waste and clean the toilets. Every monastery had a PHYSIC GARDEN where plants used in the treatment of patients would be grown. Herbs, such as peony, ginger, cinnamon and balsam, were expected to be always available to comfort the sick, and money was spent on other luxury goods such as aniseed, wine, cassis, cloves, saxifrage, liquorice, olive oil and vinegar. Monks were probably the only skilled medical personnel available to most people. Most hospitals at the time were attached to monasteries or run by monks (see page 20).

Bath-houses

Archaeological evidence also shows that many towns in the Middle Ages had bath-houses where people could pay to have a bath (see Source 1). We also know that people used combs and tweezers, toothpicks and mouthwashes. Perhaps many medieval people were, despite all the difficulties, not quite as dirty or as smelly as some textbooks suggest!

A case study of Coventry
Were all medieval towns dirty and unhealthy places to live?

Surprisingly, the answer to this question is 'no'. Dolly Jørgensen, in a recent academic paper 'What to do with waste', argues convincingly that Coventry council made a concerted and consistent effort to clean up the city.

In 1421 the Mayor's Proclamation required that every man clean the street in front of his house every Saturday or pay a twelve penny fine, with no exceptions being made. Waste collection services are recorded in 1420, when the council gave William Oteley the right to collect one penny from every resident and shop, on a quarterly basis, for his weekly street cleansing and waste removal services. The waste was to be sold to nearby farmers.

The council also specified designated waste disposal locations. DUNGHILLS and waste pits naturally sprang up around the perimeter of the town. The council authorised the use of specific sites for particular types of waste. By 1427, five designated waste-disposal locations are mentioned for Coventry (Dolly Jørgensen only specifically lists four):

- a dunghill outside of the city limit beyond Greyfriar Gate
- a pit in the Little Park Street Gate
- a muckhill near the cross situated beyond New Gate, at Derne Gate
- a pit at Poodycroft.

In total, Coventry's council banned waste disposal in the River Sherbourne nine times between 1421 and 1475. There are, of course, two ways of looking at this: that the council took action, and it was widely ignored; or, perhaps, the actions worked and when one or two individuals went back to the old ways then residents complained to the council who then took action.

Some towns, such as Shrewsbury shown here, made efforts to become clean and orderly

In 1421 all latrines over the Red Ditch, a local stream, were ordered to be removed, to allow free flowing of the water, and to prevent flooding. Attempts were made to stop local stables and butchers throwing waste into the River Sherbourne, again to prevent flooding. All this evidence shows active intervention by the mayor and Corporation of Coventry when faced with complaints by residents about the state of the town.

THINK

1 Does Dolly Jørgensen's paper on Coventry (she uses York as an example, too) prove that towns were cleaner than we think?
2 What other actions could Coventry have taken to clean itself up?

TOPIC SUMMARY

Public health in the Middle Ages
- You were more likely to die in a town than in the countryside.
- Industry and livestock alongside houses led to dirt and disease.
- Water supply and rubbish removal caused many problems.
- Most towns only took action sporadically, or when disaster threatened.
- Some people and some towns tried to keep themselves clean as best they could.

PROGRESS CHECK

Significance
1 How significant is the case of Coventry in understanding how clean British towns were at this time?

Usefulness of sources
2 How useful is Source 1 as evidence of how clean people were in the Middle Ages?

1.6 Pulling it all together: Medieval Britain

Melcombe, Dorset

A case study of the Black Death

In 1348 a ship docked at Melcombe in Dorset, bringing with it the Black Death. People must have known it was coming as it had spread INEXORABLY across the known world from Asia. Its impact was devastating. In some places whole villages were wiped out. Historians disagree about just how many people were killed by the epidemic of 1348–49, but estimates vary from 50 to 66 per cent.

THINK

1 Before reading people's thoughts on the causes of the Black Death here, look back to Topic 1.2 (pages 12–13). Which different reasons do *you* think people in the Middle Ages would have given for the Black Death?

2 What different treatments do you think they would have suggested?

3 Which of the suggested causes of the Black Death do you find surprising? Why?

4 Which of these causes do you think would help people to treat those infected by the Black Death? Which would not? Does this help to explain why the disease spread so quickly and killed so many?

What did people think caused the Black Death?

The truth is that people at the time didn't really know much at all about the causes of ill-health, but they had plenty of theories!

Bad smells, from an overflowing privy or rotting food, corrupt the air.

Invisible fumes are spreading across the country.

The Four Humours are out of balance in each victim.

God is angry with us – not enough people have been going to church or behaving properly.

The planets can explain it. Saturn is in conjunction with Mars and Jupiter and that always means something bad happens.

People have been wearing fancy new clothes, and showing off their wealth. This has made God very angry and therefore he has sent a plague, like he did in Biblical times, to teach us to behave better.

There was a huge earthquake in China in 1347, and this is where the Black Death started in 1347.

The Jews have poisoned the wells and springs.

How did people try to treat the Black Death and stop it spreading?

There were many treatments and preventions proposed, some of which were sold by those quick to make a profit.

To avoid infection:
1. *March through the streets praying to God to spare us from the Plague: by order of the King.*
2. *Protect yourself by making candles as tall as yourself, and burning them in church.*
3. *Avoid eating too much.*
4. *Avoid taking a bath as opening the pores of the skin will let in the disease.*
5. *Avoid having sex as too much excitement can weaken you and make you more likely to catch the Plague.*
6. *Avoid all Plague victims.*
7. *Clean all filth from the streets: by order of the King.*
8. *Carry a posy of sweet-smelling herbs and spices to keep away the evil smells.*
9. *Attend church and pray for your soul every day to keep you healthy.*
10. *Bathe in urine three times a day, or drink it once a day to protect you from harm.*

For those who are infected:
1. *Pop open the buboes (the swellings in the armpits) to release the disease.*
2. *Attach a live chicken (or pigeon) to the buboes to drive away the disease.*
3. *Drink a mixture of vinegar and mercury.*
4. *Carry out flagellation (walking through the streets praying to God for forgiveness and whipping yourself).*
5. *Bleeding will release the evils inside the body.*

ACTIVITY

1 Read the notices above. Rank these 'preventions' for the Black Death, and then rank the 'cures':
   a) in the order that *you* think might be effective
   b) in the order that *people at the time* might think effective.
2 Can you explain any differences between your views and the views of people at the time?

3 Why do you think there were so many different types of treatment for the Black Death?
4 Are you surprised how many people died from the Black Death?
5 What does the response to the Black Death tell us about how medieval people understood the causes of disease, and how to treat diseases effectively?

Black Death backtrack: Don't blame the rats, the plague was 'spread by PEOPLE'

(*Daily Mail*, 18 August 2011)

It is important to remember that historians today still debate the exact causes of the Black Death. The prevailing argument is that it was bubonic plague spread by rats. However, others suggest that it was spread by close contact between humans. Archaeologists just haven't found lots of rat bones, suggesting the Plague wasn't spread by rats, and the fact that mortality rose in winter suggests the Black Death may have been something other than bubonic plague all together. If *we* find it difficult to understand what caused the disease, what chance did people in the Middle Ages have of understanding the cause, and then effectively curing, such a rampant disease?

SOURCE 1

Monks with the Plague being blessed by a priest

Were people healthier in 1450?

FOCUS TASK

What happened to you if you fell ill in medieval Britain?

Now it's time to review your work on healthcare in medieval Britain. In the left-hand column of the table below you will find a list of ailments common in medieval times. You have to decide how those ailments would be treated, by whom and what the likely outcomes might be. Look back to the description of this task on pages 7–8 if you need a reminder.

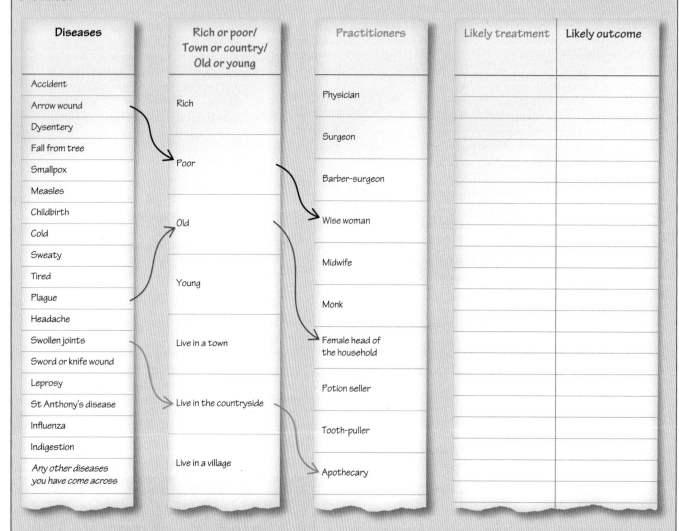

Diseases	Rich or poor/ Town or country/ Old or young	Practitioners	Likely treatment	Likely outcome
Accident	Rich	Physician		
Arrow wound				
Dysentery		Surgeon		
Fall from tree	Poor			
Smallpox		Barber-surgeon		
Measles				
Childbirth	Old	Wise woman		
Cold				
Sweaty		Midwife		
Tired	Young			
Plague		Monk		
Headache				
Swollen joints	Live in a town	Female head of the household		
Sword or knife wound				
Leprosy		Potion seller		
St Anthony's disease	Live in the countryside			
Influenza		Tooth-puller		
Indigestion				
Any other diseases you have come across	Live in a village	Apothecary		

1 Did everyone get *the same* medical treatment?
2 Did anyone get *effective* medical treatment?
3 Was medical treatment, in your opinion, any better in 1450 than it had been in 1000?

Which factors inhibited or encouraged medical change in medieval times?

As we have seen, for example with the work of John Arderne (page 17), some people were able to make improvements to the way they treated the sick during medieval times, but many were not.

FOCUS TASK

Medieval Britain factor card

Throughout your course you will be thinking about how the following factors affected the story of Health and the People. Which of these factors were significant during medieval times? We think that in medieval times the Church was of great significance so we have given it a '5'. Do you agree?

MEDIEVAL BRITAIN		
Factor	Relative importance of the factor	Positive or negative influence
War		
Superstition and religion	5	+ and –
Chance		
Government		
Communication		
Science and technology		
The economy		
Ideas		
Role of the individual		

1 Decide which factors you think are most important in explaining any changes in health that took place during medieval times. On your own copy of the factor card, give each factor a number value, where 1 is least important, and 5 most important. Remember to decide whether they are important for creating change, or for inhibiting change. In some cases, it might be both. You should also be able to explain *why* some factors were more important than others.
2 Discuss your findings in groups. Do other people in your group agree with your ideas?

KEY WORDS

Make sure you know what these words mean, and are able to use them confidently in your own writing. See the Glossary on pages 111–112 for definitions.
- Autopsy
- Cauterise
- Doctrine of signatures
- Hippocratic Oath
- Mortality
- Physic garden

The beginnings
of change

2

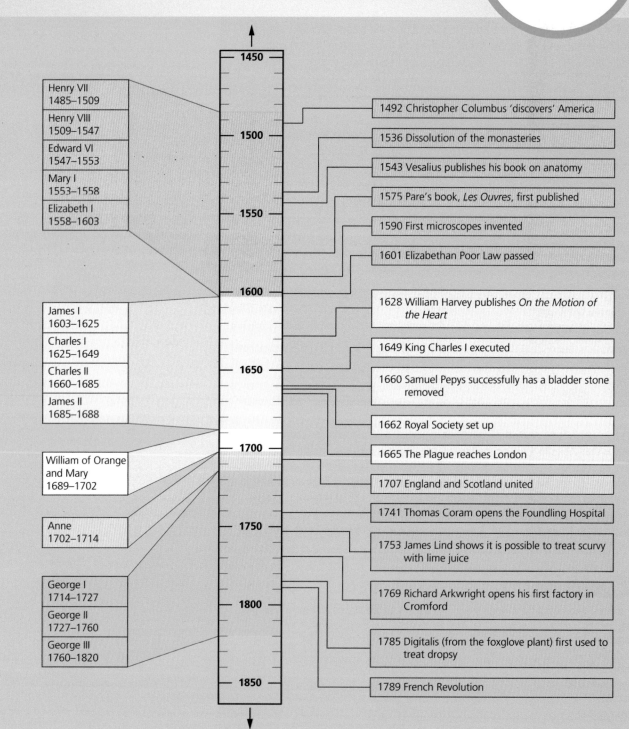

Monarchs	Timeline	Events

Henry VII
1485–1509

Henry VIII
1509–1547

Edward VI
1547–1553

Mary I
1553–1558

Elizabeth I
1558–1603

James I
1603–1625

Charles I
1625–1649

Charles II
1660–1685

James II
1685–1688

William of Orange
and Mary
1689–1702

Anne
1702–1714

George I
1714–1727

George II
1727–1760

George III
1760–1820

1450
1500
1550
1600
1650
1700
1750
1800
1850

1492 Christopher Columbus 'discovers' America

1536 Dissolution of the monasteries

1543 Vesalius publishes his book on anatomy

1575 Pare's book, *Les Ouvres*, first published

1590 First microscopes invented

1601 Elizabethan Poor Law passed

1628 William Harvey publishes *On the Motion of the Heart*

1649 King Charles I executed

1660 Samuel Pepys successfully has a bladder stone removed

1662 Royal Society set up

1665 The Plague reaches London

1707 England and Scotland united

1741 Thomas Coram opens the Foundling Hospital

1753 James Lind shows it is possible to treat scurvy with lime juice

1769 Richard Arkwright opens his first factory in Cromford

1785 Digitalis (from the foxglove plant) first used to treat dropsy

1789 French Revolution

2.1 Context: Early modern Britain

THINK

You have probably studied early modern Britain before. You may be quite an expert already. So what do you think of our visual summary of this period? Discuss these questions.

1 Do you agree with the images we have chosen to summarise early modern Britain? What do you think we have left out?
2 Which images would you use to sum up life in Britain at this time? Why?
3 How much change do you think there was between 1485 and 1800?
4 Do you think people were better off in 1800 than they were in 1485?
5 What impact do you think these changes will have had on people's health?

Andreas Vesalius, 1514–64

- Born in Brussels.
- Studied medicine at Paris and Padua.
- Became professor of surgery and anatomy at Padua.
- Carried out his own dissections.
- Believed anatomy was the key to understanding how the human body worked.
- Published *De Humani Corporis Fabrica* in 1543, which changed attitudes to medicine.

Ambroise Paré, 1510–90

- Apprenticed to his elder brother, a barber-surgeon.
- Learned much of his skill as an army surgeon.
- Used Galen's method of ligatures to seal a wound.
- He is considered one of the 'fathers of modern surgery'.

What was the Renaissance?

The Renaissance, or 'rebirth', began in northern Europe in the mid-fifteenth century. Initially, it was triggered by the rediscovery of a love of all things CLASSICAL – buildings, statues, paintings and texts. At the same time, the Reformation was challenging accepted religious ideas: Protestantism against Catholicism; Luther and Henry VIII against the Pope. This led to people challenging ideas and beliefs in science, technology and how the world was viewed. It was the beginning of what became known as 'the scientific method' and led many eminent people to question the beliefs of Galen and other classical scholars. This was to have a profound impact on many aspects of life, including health and the way diseases were diagnosed and treated.

New inventions aided this. The microscope revolutionised the work of both scientists and physicians. Inventions such as Caxton's printing press enabled the more rapid spread of ideas across Britain. The years 1500–1650 were a time of major breakthroughs in many areas, although some ideas and practices took much longer to affect the way illness was treated. Vesalius challenged Galen's works on human anatomy, and developed much more accurate views of the inside of the human body by, unlike Galen, looking at and dissecting humans rather than animals.

Being ill in the seventeenth century

The biggest killer diseases in the seventeenth century were 'fever, consumption, teeth, gripping in the guts, and convulsions'. Just the very descriptions tell us how little physicians and surgeons understood about the causes of disease, let alone cures. These diseases are not so very different from the killer diseases of the sixteenth or fifteenth centuries, or, for that matter, earlier times. And it should be no surprise to discover that the treatments offered were, in general, not so very different from before.

What has changed?

The Renaissance introduced the idea of a more scientific method, which was readily adopted by some people, and scorned by others. Ambroise Paré, a French barber-surgeon, is perhaps the most famous example from the sixteenth century of someone who adopted the new scientific ways of treating disease. He trained at the Hotel du Dieu hospital in Paris before becoming a surgeon in the French army. At the siege of Milan in 1536 he ran out of hot oil for cauterising wounds. He made up a mixture of egg yolk, turpentine and oil of roses to dress raw wounds. It was much less painful and, as he discovered the next morning, much more effective at helping healing. He also used LIGATURES to tie-off wounds after amputation instead of cauterisation, and found that wounds healed better. Later he helped develop artificial limbs for those who had lost a hand or a leg due to their wounds. His time as an army surgeon allowed Paré to observe his patients and treat them more effectively. He published his experiences in a book, *Les Oeuvres*, in 1575, and became famous across Europe.

PROGRESS CHECK

Causes and consequences

1 What changes did the Renaissance bring to health?

Significance

2 Who do you think had the greater impact, Vesalius or Paré?

Causes and factors

3 What do you think helped bring about change more, war or science and technology?

2.2 The impact of the Renaissance on Britain

FOCUS

The work of Vesalius and Paré found its way to England partly through the new books, but also through English surgeons and physicians training at European medical schools. Many studied in Italy and returned to England to spread new ideas. But some areas were resistant to change, and many people still could not afford to be treated by physicians or surgeons. This topic assesses just how much of an impact the new ideas of the Renaissance had on health.

What part did art play in improving people's health during the Renaissance?

Artists like Leonardo da Vinci went to great lengths to study the human body so they could better represent it in their drawings and paintings. They began to study corpses to help them accurately draw humans. It was a short step from that to dissecting parts of the body to see how muscles and sinews worked. Artists also illustrated the new medical books, helping to spread new knowledge and ideas.

The Renaissance and Galen

Initially, the Renaissance led to a revival of all things ancient. Many of Galen's works were retranslated into Greek and Latin. Texts were compared and efforts made to get back to the original meaning. As with buildings, art and theatre, so with medicine. Galen and his contemporaries were lionised as if they could do no wrong. By 1525 his complete works had been published in Greek, and translations into Latin soon followed. Galen was regarded as the font of all medical knowledge, to be slavishly copied.

Of course, this could not last. The very essence of the Renaissance was questioning. The more artists and surgeons studied anatomy, and the more humans they dissected, the more they began to notice discrepancies between what Galen said and what they were discovering for themselves. The initial reaction was that Galen was right, and the current anatomists were wrong. But gradually enough opinion grew to successfully challenge Galen and cast doubts on his observations. Once challenged on anatomy then other challenges followed. The medical world seemed to be split in two, depending on how strongly they supported Galen. It also seemed to split between physicians, who mostly learned from texts and lectures and thus largely supported Galen's ideas, and surgeons, who were exploring the human body on a daily basis and were learning by experiment and experience. Scientific discovery played a part in this as new tools, like the microscope, allowed both scientists and medical men to look at things in ever more detail.

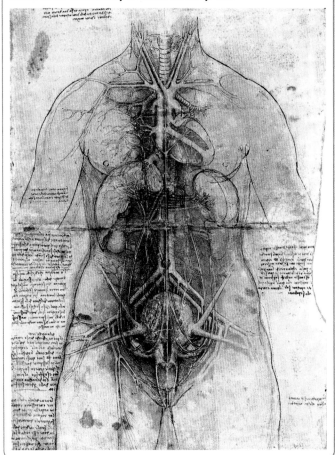

SOURCE 1

Leonardo da Vinci's study of female anatomy, 1510

THINK

1. How might Leonardo da Vinci have found out about human anatomy?
2. How does this show changing attitudes during the Renaissance?
3. How might drawings such as Source 1 help surgeons to treat sick people?

William Harvey, 1578–1657

- Born in Kent in 1578 and educated at Cambridge University.
- Studied medicine at the University of Padua in Italy.
- Returned to England in 1602 and set himself up as a physician. His career benefited from his marriage to the daughter of Elizabeth I's physician.
- Accepted a post at St Bartholomew's Hospital in 1609 and worked there for the rest of his life. Appointed physician to both James I and Charles I.

THINK

1   How was William Harvey able to prove that blood circulated around the human body?
2   Why did people oppose his work?
3   What does the story of William Harvey tell us about health and healthcare during the Renaissance?
4   Is it fair to say that William Harvey's work changed medicine for ever?

William Harvey and the circulation of blood

Harvey's most famous work, *On the Motion of the Heart,* was published in 1628. It, more than any other book at the time, challenged the work of Galen and the ancients, and changed medicine for ever.

While studying in Padua, Harvey was taught that the veins in the human body had valves, and blood pumped only one way. But no one understood how or why. Later in his career Harvey experimented on animals, and it was during this experimentation that he discovered blood was pumped around the body in a circular motion. This led to his famous discovery of the circulation of the blood.

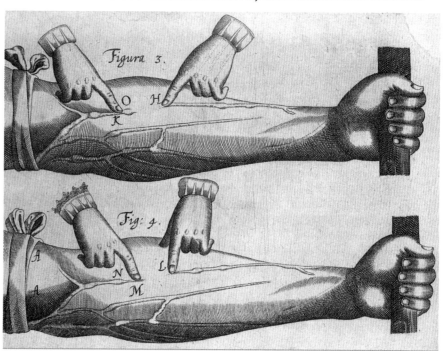

His discovery was made partly as a result of theoretical work as he was unable to actually see tiny CAPILLARIES in the bloodstream. But it was also as a result of experiment and observation. His work on cold-blooded AMPHIBIANS, whose blood circulates much more slowly, allowed him to see blood pumping around the body, and his most famous experiment, described in his book, showed blood moving in a patient's forearm. With this experiment he was able to show convincingly that the heart worked as a pump, and that blood flowed in a 'one-way system' around the human body.

He was also able to show that Galen's belief that the liver, not the heart, was the centre of the human body, was completely wrong. Galen had believed that the liver made new blood to replace that lost around the body. Harvey's work on the circulation of blood proved that this was wrong, and also challenged the idea of 'bleeding' as a cure. If Harvey was right then it was impossible for the body to have too much blood.

How was Harvey's work greeted by contemporaries?

As you might imagine, those who supported Galen totally rejected Harvey's work. They argued that Harvey could not see capillaries and therefore could not prove their existence. It would be another 60 years before capillaries were observed in action. Some refused to accept the role of experiments in challenging the ancient texts. Many were very conservative and resistant to change. In fact, Harvey himself told a friend that he lost many patients after 1628 because of his 'crack-pot ideas'.

A case study of Thomas Sydenham – the 'English Hippocrates'?

As we have seen (see page 13) Hippocrates was regarded as the 'father of modern medicine'. He argued for the need to base any treatment on examining a person as a whole, and basing decisions on observation. He also believed in exercise and moderation. So if writers have called Thomas Sydenham the 'English Hippocrates' that should give us some idea of Sydenham's thinking.

Born in 1624, Thomas Sydenham was educated at both Oxford and Cambridge universities, before joining the Parliamentary Army during the English Civil War. He set up as a physician in London in 1663, being licensed by the College of Physicians. Sydenham distrusted those who based their diagnoses and treatments on book learning. When once asked by a student which medical book he should read, Sydenham replied, *Don Quixote*. He firmly believed in close observation of the symptoms of a disease, and as little intervention as possible. He insisted physicians must avoid speculation, and carefully monitor both the symptoms and any treatments given. That way they could build up a body of knowledge based on experience. He was a strong advocate of the 'scientific method' of treating ill-health. He believed diseases had different characteristics, and thus each disease had a separate, unique treatment.

FACTFILE

Don Quixote

First published in 1605 this famous Spanish novel follows the adventures of Don Quixote as he travels around the country, righting wrongs and having adventures. It is renowned for an episode when Don Quixote tilts at windmills, thinking they are giants. It is regarded as one of the best novels written in any country at that time and would have been well-known by educated people in Britain.

He was particularly interested in treating the ague, a form of malaria, and used chinchona bark, from the tropical rainforests of South America, to successfully treat the condition. A story told about him illustrates his style as a practitioner. He had diagnosed a 'gentleman of fortune' with HYPOCHONDRIA. The patient was finally told that Sydenham could do no more for him, but that there was, living at Inverness, a certain Dr Robertson who had great skill in cases like his. The patient journeyed to Inverness full of hope and, finding no doctor of the name there, came back to London full of rage, but cured of his complaint!

Sydenham was particularly interested in smallpox and diseases which struck London as epidemics nearly every year. He developed a successful treatment for smallpox that seemed the complete opposite of what physicians usually did. They usually piled blankets on the patient and administered lots of hot drinks, trying to sweat the disease out of the body. Sydenham devised a 'cool therapy', prescribing lots of fluids, very moderate bleeding and keeping the patient as cool as possible. This treatment, with its echoes of the Four Humours (see page 13), seemed to work.

Some enlightened contemporaries hailed Sydenham and his treatments, but most people at the time thought him eccentric. Whoever heard of a doctor claiming it best not to treat a patient unnecessarily!

THINK

5   To what extent do Sydenham's ideas and treatments follow those of Hippocrates?
6   Why do you think many physicians thought him eccentric?
7   In what ways does his work:
    a)   support Galen
    b)   challenge Galen?
8   How similar, and how different, are the approaches of William Harvey and Thomas Sydenham to treating ill-health?
9   Can you explain why neither of these men had much impact on health during the time they lived?

What about the surgeons?

Operations at the time were dangerous events, which many people did not survive.

SOURCE 2

An amputation scene from a text on surgery, c1620

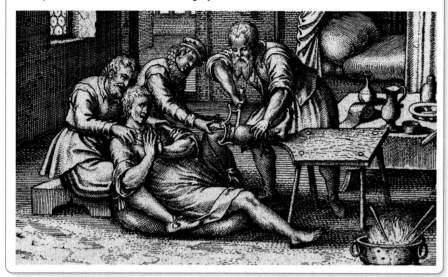

John Hunter

John Hunter was a famous surgeon and anatomist. He came to believe that the best way to heal deep wounds was to leave as much as possible to nature! He was most famous as a teacher of anatomy, training many of the best surgeons of the time, and spent many hours dissecting bodies to learn about how they worked. A recent newspaper article accused him of 'Burking' (see Factfile). He always seemed to have a fresh supply of bodies!

PROGRESS CHECK

Usefulness of sources

1 In what way does Hieronymus Fabricus alter the way we view the work of surgeons at this time?

Significance

2 Using the work of Harvey and Sydenham, what would you say was the biggest impact of the Renaissance on health?

TOPIC SUMMARY

The impact of the Renaissance on Britain

- Initially the Renaissance strengthened the ideas of Galen in the way disease should be treated.
- The Renaissance also brought a more questioning approach to the work of Galen and Hippocrates.
- Harvey and Sydenham, among others, made advances in the way people understood and treated diseases.
- Some people supported the new ideas while others opposed them, sticking closely to Galen's teachings.
- It is difficult to decide to what extent these new ideas impacted on health and the people.

SOURCE 3

By Hieronymus Fabricus, 1537–1619

I was about to cut the thigh of a man forty years of age, and ready to use the saw and cauteries. For the sick man no sooner began to roar out, but all ran away, except only my eldest son, who was then but little, and to whom I committed the holding of the thigh … and but my wife then great with child, came running out … and kept hold of the patient's chest.

THINK

1 Which do you think is more reliable in telling us about the work of surgeons, Source 2 or Source 3? Why?
2 Do these sources help us understand why surgery was so dangerous at this time?

PROFILE

John Hunter, 1728–93

- Born in Scotland.
- Moved to London as an assistant to his brother William, a successful physician.
- Served as an army surgeon during the Seven Years War where he dealt with gunshot wounds and amputations.
- Edward Jenner (see page 45) was one of his students.
- Famous in his lifetime, he was known as the 'father of scientific surgery'.

FACTFILE

'Burking' is named after William Burke and William Hare who were convicted in 1828 of committing ten murders in a few months in Edinburgh, in order to supply fresh bodies to surgeons and schools of anatomy. Hare gave evidence against Burke and therefore escaped the charge of murder. Burke, however, was hanged.

2.3 Dealing with disease

FOCUS

We have already seen how ideas about health and medicine changed during the Renaissance, and how some medical practitioners began to adopt new methods. In this topic we will look at how these changes impacted people who were ill, whether surgery improved, what new medicines were available and whether people had better access to them.

Were people more likely to survive surgery than in medieval times?

We have already seen the ways in which Ambroise Paré improved surgery (see page 32). Surgeons' skills improved too. In the 1720s William Cheselden, of St Thomas' Hospital in London, was renowned for his speed and dexterity. He was able to remove a stone from the bladder in less than a minute. There were still no reliable anaesthetics, although wine and opium began to be used widely, with unpredictable results. An incorrect dose of anaesthetic could prove fatal!

Samuel Pepys, the famous diarist, gives us an example of how many ordinary people viewed the prospect of an operation. On 26 March 1658 he underwent an operation, successful as it happens, to remove a stone from his bladder. He was so relieved to be alive afterwards that he held a celebration on 26 March every year for the rest of his life.

Fanny Burney had a mastectomy, an operation to remove a breast, in 1811. Her account gives us a vivid image of an operation from the patient's point of view (see Source 1).

SOURCE 1

Fanny Burney in a letter to her sister, Esther, in 1811

Yet – when the dreadful steel was plunged into the breast – cutting through veins – arteries – flesh – nerves – I needed no injunctions not to restrain my cries. I began a scream that lasted unintermittingly during the whole time of the incision – & I almost marvel that it rings not in my ears still! so excruciating was the agony.

Changes in the status and training of surgeons

In the eighteenth century more than half of all practising 'doctors' seem to have been men who had served an apprenticeship. As late as 1856, of the 10,220 persons listed in the *Medical Directory* with some sort of qualification, only 4 per cent had a medical degree from an English university.

Many were members of the new Royal College of Surgeons (there had been a Royal College of Physicians since 1600!) and you could only practise with a licence. No person could practise as a surgeon within seven miles of the City of London unless examined by the College. In 1811 the regulations insisted that to be a surgeon you had to attend at least one course in anatomy and one course in surgery. In 1813 it was further decreed that to be a surgeon you must have a minimum of one year's experience in a hospital. The world of the surgeon was becoming more regulated.

SOURCE 2

From *Apprenticeship Indenture, 1705* (Warwickshire County Record Office, CR 556/364)

This Indenture witnesseth that John Beale of Woolscot in the county of Warwick puts himself apprentice to William Edwards, surgeon of Kenilworth to learn his art and with him after the manner of an apprentice to serve for 4 years from this date. During the term the apprentice shall faithfully serve his master, his secrets keep, his lawful commands gladly obey; the apprentice neither to do damage to his master nor see it done; the apprentice not to waste his master's goods nor lend them unlawfully. The apprentice not to commit fornication nor contract matrimony during the term; the apprentice not to play at cards or dice or any unlawful game that may cause his master loss. The apprentice not to haunt taverns nor ale-houses nor be absent unlawfully day or night from his master's service but in all things behave as a good and faithful apprentice towards his master.

William Edwards, in consideration of the sum of £53 16s, shall teach the apprentice all the art he uses by the best means he can. William Edwards shall find the apprentice in meat, drink, washing and lodging during the term.

1 May 1705. Signatures of William Edwards, John Beale and 2 witnesses

---

THINK

1 What do the reactions of Samuel Pepys and Fanny Burney tell us about having an operation at this time?
2 Compare Fanny Burney's account of an operation (Source 1) with that of Hieronymus Fabricus (Source 3, page 36). What do they have in common? How are they different?
3 What benefits might there be to having a Royal College of Surgeons?
4 What changes had been made to the training of surgeons by 1815? How might this make them better surgeons?

Study Source 2.

5 What is expected of the surgeon?
6 What is expected of the apprentice?
7 What kind of training as a surgeon will John Beale get?
8 Do you think this is a good way to train to become a surgeon?

Medical moments in time: London, 1665

ACTIVITY

1 Look carefully at the picture. Can you identify:
   a) the surgeon
   b) the physician
   c) an example of traditional medicine
   d) a quack (see page 40)
   e) public health measures used against the Plague
   f) examples of the impact of the Renaissance on health in London in 1665?

2 Compare this picture of London in 1665 with the picture of London in 1347 (pages 22–23). Copy and complete the following table to show evidence of continuity and of change in medicine over this period.

Evidence of continuity in medicine, 1347–1665	Evidence of change in medicine, 1347–1665

3 Write a paragraph to summarise progress in health in London during the early modern period.

Plague struck in 1665. The Mayor of London ordered watchmen to guard houses to make sure the sick and their families stayed shut up.

House owners were ordered to sweep the streets outside their homes.

Taverns and theatres were closed to stop plague spreading.

It's not Plague. Your humours are out of balance, that's all. You just need bleeding.

I saw many gunshot wounds as an army doctor. I'll dig out the bullet, but it'll hurt. But we don't use boiling oil on wounds any more thanks to that Frenchman, Paré.

No meetings of the Royal Society while there's plague.

I'll miss the lectures and experiments. They're talking of transfusing blood from a dog to a man.

Hush. She's got tummy ache. Pass my copy of *New Herbal*.

The new microscopes are wonderful – detail you can't see with the naked eye.

Mother dosed us with rhubarb. It's excellent.

I like this copy of Vesalius. Good illustrations of anatomy.

Cure for the Plague! Straight from America where it saved my friend Pocahontas. One spoonful a day and you'll live to be 80.

They never had books like this before printing was invented.

I like Harvey's theory that blood circulates round the body.

Nonsense! It goes against Galen.

Even if he's right it won't help anyone who's sick.

What medicines were used in early modern Britain?

By this time most towns would have had at least one pharmacy, sometimes run by ex-monks. Most people would have continued to be treated by local wise women or with family remedies (as we saw in Chapter 1), although a market was developing in self-help medicine books.

Lady Johanna St John

Lady Johanna St John is perhaps typical of the local lady of the manor's role in healing. She lived at Lydiard House near Swindon and combined her role of running a large household with compiling a recipe book of cures. She grew many of the herbs she needed in the walled garden of Lydiard House. Her cures included the one shown in Source 3 for a bleeding nose.

It seems Lady Johanna 'collected' successful remedies from her London friends. They often sent them to Lydiard House to be made up into medicines which were then sent back to London. This went well beyond dosing up servants on the estate with traditional family treatments.

> ### SOURCE 3
> Lady Johanna St John's cure for a bleeding nose, from the seventeenth century
>
> *A sheet of white paper, wett it in vinegar and dry it in an oven – when it is dry, wett it again and dry it as before, so doing 3 times, then make it into a powder and snuff up some of it into the nose, often, as well, when it does, and when it bleeds.*

Nicholas Culpeper

Nicholas Culpeper published his *Complete Herbal* in 1653, and it is still in print today. He wrote in English, rather than Latin, in an attempt to help people and deprive physicians of what he regarded as their very inflated fees. He served as an apprentice to an apothecary in London, then set up his own shop. He treated people for free (he had married a wealthy heiress!), preferring to examine and talk to his patients in person, rather than examine their urine. Culpeper classified herbs and plants by their uses. He tried to combine the use of herbs with the Doctrine of Signatures (see page 14) and astrology, so he wasn't altogether a modernist, even if he did use herbs in a more coherent way than previously.

Ingredients from around the world

New ingredients were appearing from around the world. Rhubarb was hailed as a wonder-drug when it was first introduced from Asia. We have already come across chinchona bark from South America, and opium from China. Tobacco was brought from North America by Walter Raleigh and, despite James I writing a famous book about its evils, it quickly found many uses in herbal remedies. In fact, there is a record of some schoolboys at Eton being beaten for refusing to smoke tobacco. Apparently smoking a pipe was regarded as an excellent way to keep the Plague at bay!

> ### THINK
> 1 How easy was it for ordinary people to be treated at this time?
> 2 How effective, in your opinion, were these treatments?

Quackery

In seventeenth- and eighteenth-century Britain there was a huge increase in people inventing and selling medicines. In a time when it was difficult to know both what caused disease or what cured it, the market was wide open for people to take advantage. Quacks, after the Dutch word 'quacksalver' (someone who boasts loudly about his cures) sold medicines fully understanding that they did not do what they said they did – or if they did it was quite by accident! Quack medicine was sold both as a preventative and a cure, usually with a long list of unproven claims. It was often sold by itinerant salesmen (as in Source 4 on page 41) who had moved on before purchasers realised their product didn't work!

One famous seventeenth-century cure, 'Daffy's Elixir', was invented by a Leicestershire clergyman in 1647. He claimed it cured, among other things; 'convulsion fits, consumption, agues, piles, fits, children's distempers, worms, gout, rheumatism, kidney stones, colic and griping of the bowels', all common ailments of the time. It made him and his family a fortune, and continued to be sold across Britain and the Empire until the nineteenth century when regulation of medicines was finally introduced into Britain. Its main ingredient was brandy, along with aniseed, raisins, cochineal, fennel seed, jalap, parsley seed, rhubarb, saffron, senna, and Spanish liquorice. The best that could be said for it is that it might do you no harm, but recent medical research has shown that it would make a perfect laxative, so at least it might cure constipation!

SOURCE 4

A seller of quack cures in a medieval town, offering bottles of his remedies. Drawn in 1910

As well as alcohol the other main ingredient in quack medicines was usually opium. Both alcohol and opium would dull any pain and make the patient feel a little better, even if no cure was possible.

Success at quackery often depended on the seller's personal charm and charisma – how effectively they could play upon people's fears and uncertainty, perhaps in times of plague or epidemic. It might also depend on good packaging or an influential client such as 'Turlington's Balsam of Life', which was given a royal patent by King George II in 1744, despite being completely useless in the treatment of 'kidney and bladder stones, colic, and inward weakness' as Turlington claimed. Having a patron like the King did wonders for sales. The growth of regional and national newspapers also made it possible to advertise a product much more widely and thus create a bigger market.

> **THINK**
>
> 3 Why were quacks able to produce and sell medicine that was, in effect, useless?
> 4 Why did people buy these medicines?
> 5 What does this tell us about health and medicine at this time?

New ideas and treatments

The growth of hospitals

Thomas Coram, a retired sea captain, was the driving force behind the Foundling Hospital, opened in 1741 to provide care for abandoned children. He was shocked by the sight of so many children left on the streets. Most were babies born out of wedlock, whose mothers were in no position to care for them and continue working. He spent over ten years collecting the funds to build the new hospital, raising money from the great and good in the process.

There were many more applicants than places available, showing the desperate need for this kind of care. Babies were chosen for a place by a form of lottery. The Hospital arranged for foster families, many in the Home Counties, to care for the babies and young children until the age of five. They were then brought to live and be educated in the Foundling Hospital until the age of fifteen, many being trained for domestic or military service. The Hospital features in Jacqueline Wilson's novel *Hetty Feather*, where at the start of the story Hetty Feather returns to the Foundling Hospital after being fostered until she was five years old.

Voluntary hospitals

Other voluntary hospitals started to appear in the early eighteenth century, usually funded from INHERITANCES or private subscriptions, to fill the gap left by the abolition of the monasteries. These hospitals were rather different places to those of the medieval period. They no longer merely provided somewhere to stay and rest, but began to implement the new ways of treating the sick. Many of the people you have studied in this chapter worked in hospitals and developed their new ideas of dealing with disease while working there, although nurses were still untrained and usually unskilled.

> **THINK**
>
> 1 What do you think it would be like as a five-year-old living in a hospital like the one shown in Source 5?

SOURCE 5

The Foundling Hospital in London in the eighteenth century

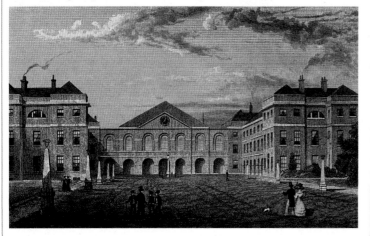

SOURCE 6

A modern-day artist's impression of James Lind treating a sailor for scurvy

New discoveries

The scientific approach to medicine brought not just new ingredients for herbal medicines but also new ideas on how to deal with disease.

- Robert Burton published a study of mental illness in 1621. He blamed lack of exercise, idleness, excessive pleasure and too much studying, among other causes, for melancholy, as the disease was known. He recommended fresh air, exercise, music and laughter as the remedy.
- In 1671 Jane Sharp published *The Midwives Book*, which combines the medical knowledge of the time with personal anecdotes. She argued that the profession of midwifery should be reserved for women, at a time when men were taking over the trade. Her practical advice was widely read and used.
- Sir John Floyer published his *A Treatise on Asthma* in 1698. He was the first to identify the causes of the disease and offer a regime for treating it, including clean air and diet.
- George Cheyne published *An Essay on Health and Long Life* in 1724. It was enormously successful and made him famous. He argued that obesity and nervous disorders were caused by HEREDITY and poor lifestyle. He argued people should take responsibility for their own health, and prevent illness, rather than rely on doctors to cure them once they became ill.
- In 1753 James Lind came up with a cure for scurvy – a disease especially prevalent among sailors on long voyages who were deprived of fresh fruit and vegetables. Scurvy killed more British sailors than war. This explains why English sailors were nicknamed 'limeys' as they were made to drink lime juice every day to stop catching scurvy!

SOURCE 7

Bill of Mortality, London, 21–28 February 1664

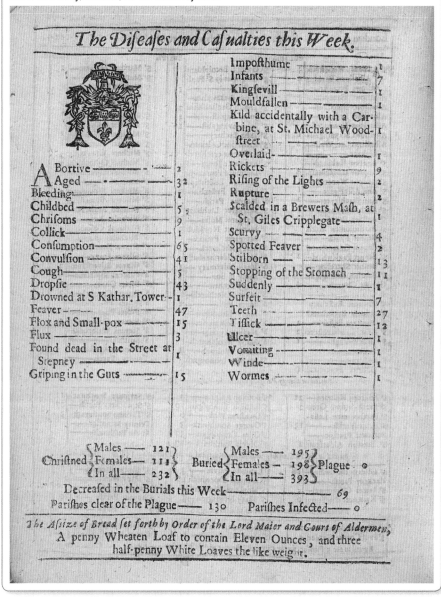

The Diseases and Casualties this Week.

Impofthume	1
Infants	7
Kingfevill	1
Mouldfallen	1
Kild accidentally with a Carbine, at St. Michael Wood-ftreet	1
Overlaid	1
Abortive	2
Aged	32
Bleeding	1
Childbed	5
Chrifoms	9
Collick	1
Confumption	65
Convulfion	41
Cough	5
Dropfie	43
Drowned at S Kathar. Tower	1
Feaver	47
Flox and Small-pox	15
Flux	3
Found dead in the Street at Stepney	1
Griping in the Guts	15
Rickets	9
Rifing of the Lights	2
Rupture	2
Scalded in a Brewers Mafh, at St. Giles Cripplegate	1
Scurvy	4
Spotted Feaver	2
Stilborn	13
Stopping of the Stomach	11
Suddenly	1
Surfeit	7
Teeth	27
Tiffick	12
Ulcer	1
Vomiting	1
Winde	1
Wormes	1

Chriftned { Males — 121, Females — 111, In all — 232 }
Buried { Males — 195, Females — 198, In all — 393 } Plague 0
Decreafed in the Burials this Week — 69
Parifhes clear of the Plague — 130   Parifhes Infected — 0

The Affize of Bread fet forth by Order of the Lord Maier and Court of Aldermen, A penny Wheaten Loaf to contain Eleven Ounces, and three half-penny White Loaves the like weight.

2 Look carefully at the Bill of Mortality for London, February 1664 (Source 7). Which are:
   a) the diseases that kill the most people
   b) the diseases that kill the least people?
3 How has this list changed since medieval times?
4 What happened to the population of London in the week 21–28 February 1664? What does that tell us about how healthy life in London was?
5 Why does the Bill of Mortality refer to 'the Plague'? What was the impact of the Plague in that week?

PROGRESS CHECK

Usefulness of sources

1 Look back to Fanny Burney's account of an operation (Source 1, page 37) and the account of Hieronymus Fabricus (Source 3, page 36). Which of the two sources helps us understand the dangers of surgery most?

Causes and consequences

2 What impact did scientific enquiry and advance have on the way most sick people were treated at this time?

Now write an answer to this question:

3 To what extent did the medical profession become better able to deal with disease in early modern Britain?

TOPIC SUMMARY

Dealing with disease

● People were more likely to survive surgery than in earlier times, although it was still very risky.
● New medicines were introduced to Britain from around the world.
● Printing meant it was easier to spread new ideas.
● Many health professionals still opposed changes to their practices.
● Most people still had very limited access to medical treatment.

FOCUS

Perhaps prevention of disease is the biggest success story of this period. The story of Edward Jenner is inspirational – an educated guess, based on experiment and scientific method, produces a vaccine that protects people from one of the most deadly infectious diseases of the period. Yet Jenner was ridiculed as a country doctor, and VACCINATION questioned as an effective method of controlling smallpox. This topic examines Jenner's findings and examines why vaccination is still a controversial issue today.

2.4 Prevention of disease – a global success story?

The MMR debate

In 1998 Dr Andrew Wakefield published a paper in the *Lancet*, the British medical journal, suggesting there was a clear link between the MMR (measles, mumps and rubella) vaccine routinely given to all young children and autism (a disorder of the brain). It claimed that evidence from his small study showed that being vaccinated with the MMR vaccine led, in some cases, to the development of autism. Even though they were only preliminary results, unverified by any other researcher, the press made a huge story out of it, and the proportion of parents having their children vaccinated plummeted. To be successful 95 per cent of the target population must be vaccinated, otherwise there is a chance of someone with the disease passing it on to others, and an epidemic can break out. Since then a fierce debate about vaccination has raged, both here in the UK and around the world.

Dr Wakefield's study has since been rejected by the medical world, and shown to be bad science. But it has led to many people distrusting *all* vaccines and the re-emergence of some diseases the World Health Organization had declared eliminated.

SOURCE 1

A poster from the 1870s against the Vaccination Law

MEN AND WOMEN OF THE TOWER HAMLETS,

And all who value Parental Liberty!

....

MR. THOMAS ERNEST WISE

Of 31 Clayhill Road, Bow

HAS BEEN IMPRISONED

for 10 days at the behest of the

VILE, FILTHY, VACCINATION LAW.

....

HE WILL BE

LIBERATED ON SATURDAY, SEPT. 27th.

Mr. WISE has been fighting a battle for freedom on behalf of Thousands of parents.

****

It is intended to give Mr. WISE a warm welcome on his return home, and to show him that We honour

Our First Vaccination Martyr.

SOURCE 2

A modern cartoon warning of the dangers of refusing vaccination

Smallpox

Smallpox is an acute contagious disease caused by the variola virus. It was one of the world's most devastating diseases. It was declared eradicated in 1980 following a global vaccination campaign led by the World Health Organization. But in earlier times it was an absolute killer. Between 30 and 60 per cent of those who caught smallpox died. Survivors carried the legacy of smallpox for life. Some were left blind; virtually all were disfigured by scars. Smallpox had long been ENDEMIC in Britain, and was a feared killer since the seventeenth century. Major epidemics killed at least 35,000 in 1796, and 42,000 between 1837 and 1840. The disease was no respecter of rank: Queen Mary died of smallpox in 1694. People thought it was created by miasma, or 'bad air'.

THINK

1 What do Sources 1 and 2 have in common?
2 How are they different?
3 What do they add to our understanding of the anti-vaccination campaign?
4 Do you think everyone should be vaccinated?

Vaccination is not new to Britain – it dates from the eighteenth century. INOCULATION had been used long before that, being widely used in the Far East for many centuries. Lady Mary Montagu came across it in Istanbul and introduced it to England in 1721. Her husband had been ambassador to the Ottoman Empire and she had seen it used there. She had personally survived a smallpox outbreak that killed her brother and left her scarred. The inoculation basically involved a mild form of smallpox being introduced into a scratch made between finger and thumb. The person being inoculated then developed a mild form of the disease, but became IMMUNE to the stronger version of smallpox. When smallpox broke out in England Lady Montagu had her children inoculated – and it worked.

A country doctor changes everything…

Edward Jenner, a country doctor in Gloucestershire who had studied in London, heard the local gossips say that milkmaids who caught cowpox never seemed to catch smallpox. He reasoned that having cowpox gave them immunity from smallpox, but how could he prove it? He experimented on local people. He chose a nine-year-old boy, James Phipps, who had had neither cowpox nor smallpox. He injected him with pus from the sores of a milkmaid with cowpox. James developed cowpox. Later, when he had recovered, Jenner gave him a dose of smallpox. James was immune. Jenner had proved that an injection of cowpox stopped people catching smallpox. He knew it worked, but didn't know how! He submitted a paper to the Royal Society in 1797 but was told he needed more proof. So he carried out more experiments, including on his own eleven-month-old son, all the time keeping detailed notes and records. Finally, in 1798 Jenner published *An Inquiry into the Causes and Effects of the Varioae Vaccinae, Or Cow-Pox*. He continued to work on vaccination and in 1802 was awarded £10,000 by the Government for his work, and a further £20,000 in 1807 after the Royal College of Physicians confirmed how effective vaccination was.

What impact did vaccination have on smallpox?

Reaction to Jenner and his work was mixed. Those who charged up to £20 a time to inoculate patients felt that their livelihoods were threatened, and poured scorn on the whole idea of change. Many people felt it was wrong to inject cowpox into humans. Some argued that smallpox was God's punishment for living a sinful life and so we should not interfere, or limit the spread of the disease. Others thought it should be up to parents to decide whether their children should be treated or not. Yet others, both for and against vaccination, felt strongly it was not the Government's job to interfere in such things.

In 1840, partly as a result of the dreadful smallpox epidemic of 1837–40, vaccination was made free to all infants, and in 1853 it was made COMPULSORY, but not strictly enforced. It seems strange that a *LAISSEZ-FAIRE* government, which was reluctant to interfere in most aspects of people's lives, would make vaccination compulsory. This, surely, tells us a lot about the fear of smallpox as a killer disease. There was an anti-vaccine league set up in England in 1866, to oppose the idea of compulsory vaccination (see Source 1, page 44). It was not until 1871 that the Government decreed parents could be fined for not having their children vaccinated. In 1887, once the death rate had fallen dramatically, the Government introduced the right for parents to refuse vaccination.

In the twentieth century, what were once endemic diseases and childhood killers such as polio, measles, diphtheria and whooping cough have almost been eliminated through vaccination programmes and the work of people like Koch and Erhlich.

THINK

5 Why was smallpox so deadly?
6 What is the difference between inoculation and vaccination?

Study Source 3.

7 How successful was vaccination in preventing smallpox:
   a) in 1870
   b) in 1870–1900
   c) after 1900
   d) today?
8 Is vaccination a 'success story'?
9 Why do you think the Government made vaccination against smallpox compulsory in 1852?

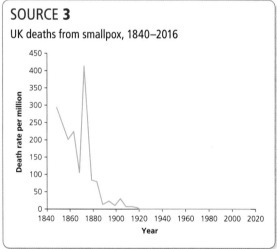

SOURCE 3

UK deaths from smallpox, 1840–2016

FACTFILE

Disease eradication

The World Health Organization has led the campaign to eliminate endemic and childhood diseases throughout the world. The last known case of smallpox was in Somalia in 1977.

What can a visit to a cemetery tell us about disease prevention?

SOURCE 4

A gravestone in Great Hale Cemetery, Lincolnshire

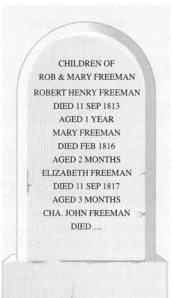

CHILDREN OF
ROB & MARY FREEMAN

ROBERT HENRY FREEMAN
DIED 11 SEP 1813
AGED 1 YEAR
MARY FREEMAN
DIED FEB 1816
AGED 2 MONTHS
ELIZABETH FREEMAN
DIED 11 SEP 1817
AGED 3 MONTHS
CHA. JOHN FREEMAN
DIED ...

SOURCE 5

A woman in labour, 1707, assisted by a midwife and attendants

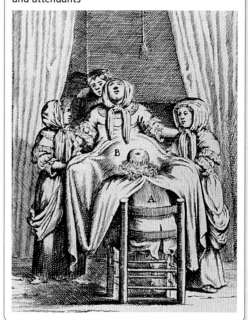

THINK

1 Look carefully at Source 4. What can you discover about the Freeman children from the gravestone?
2 What does this gravestone tell us about life:
   a) as a child a long time ago
   b) in Great Hale in Georgian times
   c) in England in Georgian times?
3 Now study Source 5. Can you identify any factors likely to cause either harm or death to the mother or newborn child?
4 Can some of these factors explain your findings in question 2?

Child-bed fever

Alexander Gordon was a naval surgeon who worked in London for several years before returning to his native Aberdeen. While there he studied an outbreak of child-bed fever and worked out what caused these deaths. He noticed that women in outlying villages who were treated by the village wise woman or midwife rarely caught the fever, whereas those treated by doctors or midwives moving from patient to patient were much more likely to die. He realised that he himself was responsible for some of the deaths. His proposed cure was simple: medical practitioners ought to wash their clothes frequently, and wash their hands in chlorinated water to try to limit the spread of disease. When he published his results in 1795 he was derided by the whole of the medical profession and it was many years before his ideas were implemented.

PROGRESS CHECK

Causes and factors

1 Which factor was more important: chance, government, science and technology or the role of the individual, in the discovery of a cure for smallpox?

Significance

2 How does the work of Jenner help us to understand the world of medicine in early modern Britain?

Now, write an answer to this question:

3 Did medical advances in early modern Britain reduce child mortality?

TOPIC SUMMARY

Prevention of disease

- Edward Jenner discovered how to stop people catching smallpox.
- The Government eventually made vaccination compulsory.
- Smallpox was virtually eliminated as a killer disease in just a few years.
- Many people opposed the idea of compulsory vaccination, and still do today.
- Vaccination is a worldwide success story, as many killer diseases have been eliminated.
- Child mortality remained high, with around 30 per cent of children dying before the age of five.

2.5 Pulling it all together:
Early modern Britain

A case study of London in 1665

Plague came often to major towns and cities. In 1604, 30 per cent of the population of York died in an outbreak of the Plague. In 1665 around 100,000 people died of the Plague in London – that was nearly 25 per cent of the population. Other towns and cities were affected too. Most doctors fled, fearing for their lives. Wealthy people left the city for their country houses until the Plague had gone, but in many cases that just spread the Plague to new places. Studying the Plague, and how people reacted to it, gives us a great opportunity to decide how much had changed between the Black Death in 1348–49 and the Plague in 1665.

What did people think caused the Plague?

The truth is that people didn't really know much at all about the causes of the Plague, but they had plenty of theories. On the right is a picture of a plague doctor wearing the protective outfit designed by Charles de Lorme in Italy in 1619.

People did notice that there were more Plague victims in the poorer and dirtier parts of London, so were beginning to make the links between dirt and disease. The King of England and the Mayor of London introduced a series of measures to try to prevent the spread of the disease.

To prevent the Plague:
- All public entertainment to be stopped.
- Pigs and other animals are not to be kept in the city.
- All dogs and cats are to be caught and killed.
- Rubbish must be cleared from the streets.
- Fires are to be lit in the streets, to drive away 'bad' air.
- Houses containing Plague victims are to be sealed up for 40 days and the door painted with a red cross.
- No strangers are to be let into the city without a certificate of health.
- Bodies are to be buried after dark, and not in churches or churchyards.
- Public prayers are to be said on Wednesdays and Fridays.
- Weekly fasts must be held.

Nose cone full of sweet-smelling herbs

Mask

Stick

Pink-tinted glass in the face mask

Stout hat with wide brim

Very thick waxed gown

Stout gloves

Amulet (jewellery to ward off evil spirits) hidden under sleeve of coat

Stout boots

THINK

1. Look closely at the plague doctor's clothes and equipment. What do they tell you about what people at the time thought caused the Plague?
2. Look back at page 26 on what people in medieval Britain thought caused the Black Death in 1348.
3. From your work in this chapter, which of these causes do you think people in 1665 still believed caused the Plague?
4. How effective do you think these measures were at stopping the spread of the Plague in London?
5. Look back to the measures adopted to try to stop the Black Death in 1348. What are the similarities and the differences?
6. What do the differences tell us about changes in health between the 1300s and the 1600s?

What was the impact of the Plague?

THINK

1 Study Source 1. Compare the deaths in August 1665 with those of February 1664 (Source 7, page 43). How has this list changed between 1664 and 1665? Is it just the Plague that has increased its number of victims?

2 What happened to the population of London in the week 15–22 August 1665?

3 What does this tell us about the impact of the Plague?

4 What does the extract from Pepys' diary (Source 2) add to our understanding of the Plague?

SOURCE 1

Bill of Mortality, London, 15–22 August 1665

The Diseases and Casualties this Week.

A Bortive	6	Kingsevil	10
Aged	54	Lethargy	1
Apoplexie	1	Murthered at Stepney	1
Bedridden	1	Palsie	2
Cancer	2	Plague	3880
Childbed	23	Plurisie	1
Chrisomes	15	Quinsie	6
Collick	1	Rickets	23
Consumption	174	Rising of the Lights	19
Convulsion	88	Rupture	2
Dropsie	40	Sciatica	1
Drowned 2, one at St. Kath. Tower, and one at Lambeth	2	Scowring	13
Feaver	353	Scurvy	1
Fistula	1	Sore legge	1
Flox and Small-pox	10	Spotted Feaver and Purples	190
Flux	2	Starved at Nurse	1
Found dead in the Street at St.Bartholomew the Less	1	Stilborn	8
Frighted	1	Stone	2
Gangrene	1	Stopping of the stomach	16
Gowt	1	Strangury	1
Grief	1	Suddenly	1
Griping in the Guts	74	Surfeit	87
Jaundies	3	Teeth	113
Imposthume	18	Thrush	3
Infants	21	Tissick	6
Kild by a fall down stairs at St. Thomas Apostle	1	Ulcer	2
		Vomiting	7
		Winde	8
		Wormes	18

Christned { Males — 83. Females — 83. In all — 166 }
Buried { Males — 2656 Females — 2663 In all — 5319 } Plague — 3880.

Increased in the Burials this Week — 1289.
Parishes clear of the Plague — 34. Parishes Infected — 96.

The Assize of Bread set forth by Order of the Lord Maior and Court of Aldermen.
A penny Wheaten Loaf to contain Nine Ounces and a half, and three half-penny White Loaves the like weight.

SOURCE 2

An extract from Samuel Pepys' diary

16 October 1665. But Lord, how empty the streets are, and melancholy, so many poor sick people in the streets, full of sores, and so many sad stories overheard as I walk, everybody talking of this dead, and that man sick, and so many in this place, and so many in that. And they tell me that in Westminster there is never a physitian [sic], and but one apothecary left, all being dead – but that there are great hopes of a great decrease this week. God send it.

Were people healthier in 1800?

This is what some contemporaries had to say about medical treatments:

SOURCE 3

Bishop Latimer, in a sermon, 1552

Physic is a remedy for rich folk and not for poor: for the poor man is not able to wage the physician.

SOURCE 4

Nicholas Culpeper, 1649

All the nation are already physicians. If you ail anything, everyone you meet, whether a man or a woman, will prescribe you a medicine for it.

THINK

5   In what ways do the views of Bishop Latimer (Source 3) and Nicholas Culpeper (Source 4) agree with what you have discovered in this chapter? What do they tell us about health at this time?

FOCUS TASK

What happened to you if you fell ill in early modern Britain?

Now it's time to review your work on healthcare in early modern Britain. Below in the left-hand column you will find a list of ailments common in early modern times. All you have to do is decide how those ailments would be treated, by whom and what the likely outcomes might be.

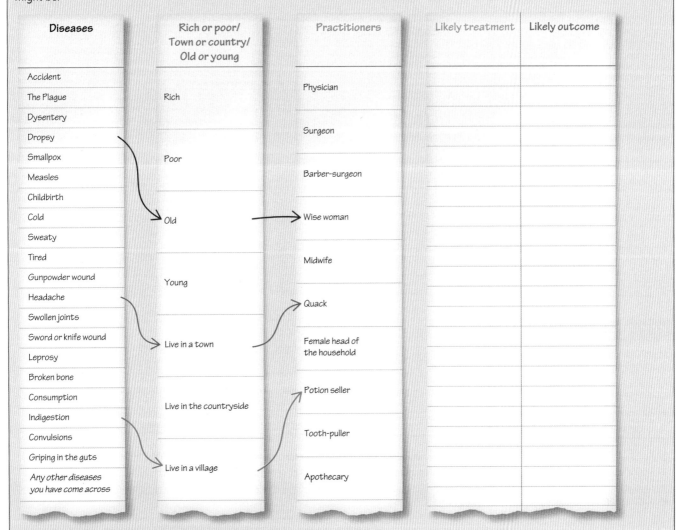

Diseases	Rich or poor/ Town or country/ Old or young	Practitioners	Likely treatment	Likely outcome
Accident		Physician		
The Plague	Rich			
Dysentery		Surgeon		
Dropsy				
Smallpox	Poor			
Measles		Barber-surgeon		
Childbirth				
Cold	Old	Wise woman		
Sweaty				
Tired		Midwife		
Gunpowder wound	Young			
Headache		Quack		
Swollen joints				
Sword or knife wound	Live in a town	Female head of the household		
Leprosy				
Broken bone		Potion seller		
Consumption	Live in the countryside			
Indigestion		Tooth-puller		
Convulsions				
Griping in the guts	Live in a village	Apothecary		
Any other diseases you have come across				

1   Did everyone get *the same* medical treatment in this period?
2   Did anyone get *effective* medical treatment in this period?
3   Was medical treatment, in your opinion, any better in 1800 than it had been in 1600? Or in 1000?

Which factors inhibited or encouraged medical change at this time?

During the course of this chapter you have come across many innovations and changes. Many of them, like Jenner's vaccination against smallpox, seem to have been greeted with dismay by much of the medical profession. Why is it that the profession was so resistant to change?

The early modern period saw many changes take place and it is true to say that the Church was much less influential during this period than in medieval times. Training and education for physicians and surgeons improved greatly, and new charitable hospitals appeared, replacing the monasteries dissolved by Henry VIII. But to what extent had the whole medical profession changed?

FOCUS TASK

Early modern Britain factor card

Throughout your course you will be thinking about how the following factors affected the story of Health and the People. Which of these factors were significant during the early modern period? We think that in the early modern period science and technology was important in bringing about change as science saw the development of new instruments such as the microscope, and new treatments, such as vaccination. Do you agree?

EARLY MODERN BRITAIN		
Factor	Relative importance of the factor	Positive or negative influence
War		
Superstition and religion		
Chance		
Government		
Communication		
Science and technology	5	+
The economy		
Ideas		
Role of the individual		

1 On your own copy of the factor card decide which factors you think are most important in explaining any changes in health that took place during early modern times. Give each factor a number value, where 1 is least important, and 5 most important. Remember to decide whether they are important for creating change, or for inhibiting change. In some cases, it might be both. You should also be able to explain *why* some factors were more important than others.
2 Discuss your findings in groups. Do other people in your group agree with your ideas?

KEY WORDS

Make sure you know what these words mean, and are able to use them confidently in your own writing. See the Glossary on pages 111–112 for definitions.
- Capillaries
- Empiricism
- Endemic
- Epidemics
- Immune
- Ligature
- Vaccination

A revolution in medicine, c1800–c1900

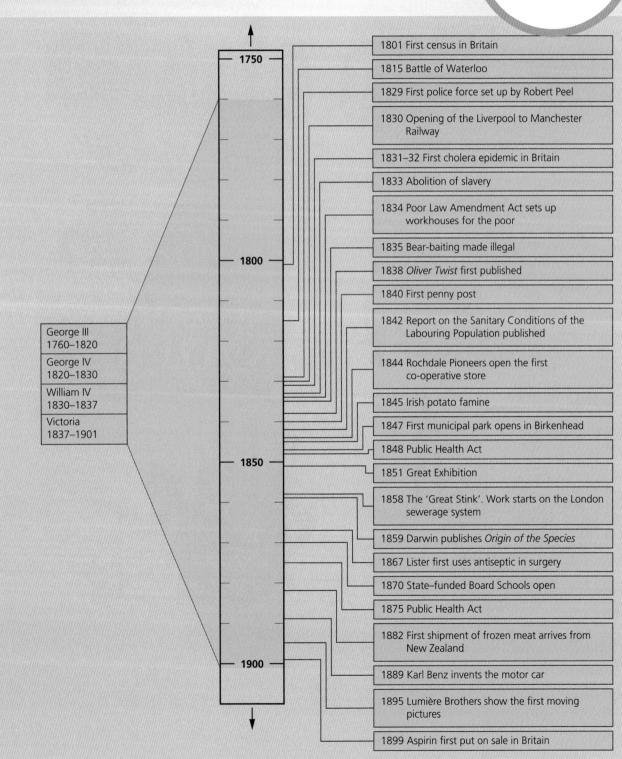

George III 1760–1820

George IV 1820–1830

William IV 1830–1837

Victoria 1837–1901

1750

1800

1850

1900

1801 First census in Britain

1815 Battle of Waterloo

1829 First police force set up by Robert Peel

1830 Opening of the Liverpool to Manchester Railway

1831–32 First cholera epidemic in Britain

1833 Abolition of slavery

1834 Poor Law Amendment Act sets up workhouses for the poor

1835 Bear-baiting made illegal

1838 *Oliver Twist* first published

1840 First penny post

1842 Report on the Sanitary Conditions of the Labouring Population published

1844 Rochdale Pioneers open the first co-operative store

1845 Irish potato famine

1847 First municipal park opens in Birkenhead

1848 Public Health Act

1851 Great Exhibition

1858 The 'Great Stink'. Work starts on the London sewerage system

1859 Darwin publishes *Origin of the Species*

1867 Lister first uses antiseptic in surgery

1870 State–funded Board Schools open

1875 Public Health Act

1882 First shipment of frozen meat arrives from New Zealand

1889 Karl Benz invents the motor car

1895 Lumière Brothers show the first moving pictures

1899 Aspirin first put on sale in Britain

3.1 Context: Nineteenth-century Britain

THINK

You have probably studied nineteenth-century Britain before. You may be quite an expert already.
So what do you think of our visual summary of this period? Discuss these questions.

1   Do you agree with the images we have chosen to summarise nineteenth-century Britain?
    What do you think we have left out?
2   Which images would you use to sum up life in Britain at this time? Why?
3   How much change do you think there was between 1800 and 1900?
4   Do you think people were better off in 1900 than they were in 1800?
5   What impact do you think these changes had on people's health?

An industrial revolution?

Many historians call the nineteenth century a time of 'great changes'. Population grew rapidly, as you can see from Source 1. Where people lived changed too. After 1851 more people lived in towns than in the countryside, and more people worked in industry than in agriculture. The source of wealth also changed as industry and trade became a quicker route to riches than owning land. ENTREPRENEURS and successful businessmen started to buy up old landed estates and take their place in running the country. Many argued that their spectacular wealth was made by exploiting their workers, forcing them to work long hours for very low wages.

Life in towns

The new towns that grew so rapidly during the century were pretty squalid places in which to live, and, increasingly, this led to demands for action to be taken. Conflicting theories emerged. One, espoused by people like Jeremy Bentham and Samuel Smiles (the author of the best-selling book, *Self Help*), maintained that it was *not* the business of government to intervene in social conditions or in the relationship between workers and employers. Others, such as Edwin Chadwick, Lord Shaftesbury, Octavia Hill and Elizabeth Fry, argued that the state had *a duty* to interfere, and to put right the wrongs of society. This was an argument that reverberated around society for most of the century, and is still pertinent today.

Much of the infrastructure of society changed. Technology brought the 'Penny Post' (the first postal system); the telegraph; cheap transport using the new railways and, towards the end of the century, popular newspapers like the *Daily Mail*. It was now possible to travel quickly and cheaply and for the first time find out what was happening in London and other parts of the country within 24 hours. News travelled fast!

Changes in healthcare

There were also 'great changes' in medicine. People like Pasteur and Koch (see pages 54–55) completely altered the way we understand diseases and how they spread. Great investigative work by people like Snow (see page 67) helped conquer the killer disease of cholera, and a new industry manufacturing medical remedies grew up later in the nineteenth century. Also during this period, Florence Nightingale played a large role in improving the care sick people received in hospitals. And yet, when the Boer War broke out in 1899, thousands of volunteers were rejected. In some towns 90 per cent of volunteers were found to be unfit to serve in the army. So what impact had this 'revolution in medicine' had on ordinary people and their health? And were people healthier in 1900 than in 1800?

SOURCE 1

Population of Great Britain and Ireland, 1801–1901. Taken from *Whitaker's Almanac*, 1941

Year	Population
1801	16.3m
1811	18.5m
1821	20.9m
1831	24.1m
1841	26.8m
1851	27.5m
1861	29.1m
1871	31.7m
1881	35.1m
1891	37.8m
1901	41.6m

FACTFILE

The Boer War, 1899–1902

In 1899 war broke out between some of the people of the British colony of South Africa and Britain. The Boers, mostly of Dutch origin, wanted to be free of British rule. They fought a guerrilla-style war, and managed to inflict heavy casualties on the British before ending the war in 1902.

THINK

6   Study Source 1. When did the population grow fastest?

7   Is a rising population a good thing, or a bad thing?

8   What impact on nineteenth-century Britain did the rise in population have?

9   Why, in your opinion, were the new towns and cities such unhealthy places to live?

10 Do you think the nineteenth century was an exciting time to live?

11 Were people healthier in 1900 than in 1800? Which of the events on the timeline (page 51), in your opinion, might help make people healthier?

12 How is it possible to have a 'revolution in medicine' and yet have so many men so unfit that they could not join the army?

3.2 The development of germ theory and its impact on the treatment of disease

FOCUS

At the beginning of the nineteenth century most people still believed ill-health was caused by bad air, the 'spontaneous combustion' of disease or an imbalance of the Four Humours. Germ theory changed all that. By the 1880s and 1890s huge steps had been taken in identifying the cause of disease, thus enabling techniques to be developed to effectively treat illnesses. This topic explores the real optimism people had in this period in the power of medical science to discover treatments and transform the hold diseases had over society.

A scientific revolution?

Three people played a major part in this breakthrough: Pasteur, Koch and Ehrlich. They were not the only ones, but they led the way in experimental science. Louis Pasteur was French, and was the first person to establish the link between germs and disease. He argued that micro-organisms were responsible for disease, and that if only we could discover these micro-organisms then a vaccine could be developed to specifically target the disease. This allowed him to develop effective vaccines to target specific diseases. His first work was on chicken cholera, and this led in 1880 to an effective vaccine against rabies.

Robert Koch, a German, took this work further. In the laboratory he was able to link particular germs to particular diseases. In 1882 he identified the specific BACILLUS that caused tuberculosis, and in 1883 and 1884 those responsible for cholera, thus confirming the work of John Snow in Britain in 1854 (see page 67). Following this he and his students rapidly isolated the causes of many diseases including diphtheria, typhoid, pneumonia, plague, tetanus and whooping cough, all of which were major killer diseases in Britain.

Paul Ehrlich was one of Koch's students. He epitomises the scientific approach to identifying and treating diseases. He is perhaps best known for Salvarsan 606, developed in 1910, as the first effective treatment for syphilis, an STD that was widespread at the time. It was called '606' because it was literally the 606th drug he and his colleagues had used to try to kill the germs causing syphilis. Salvarsan 606 was the first of what became known as 'magic bullets', carefully designed drugs targeting the specific germs causing that illness, and having little or no effect on any other part of the human body. No wonder people were so excited about the power of science to eradicate disease!

Science helped in other ways too. The stethoscope, invented in Paris in 1816 for listening to breathing ailments, became widely used from 1850 onwards, as well as thermometers, more powerful microscopes and even the first X-ray machine invented in 1895. The first clinical trials were held as scientists realised that proof of their successes came from large numbers of results. Training improved. The French physiologist Pierre Cabanis was often quoted as saying physicians should 'read little, see much, and do much'. In other words, the key to good medicine is careful observation, careful experiment and careful recording of the results. There was increasing specialisation within medicine, with one of the most important specialisms from 1850 onwards being tropical medicine. With the increased European presence in Africa, long known as the 'White Man's Grave', attempts were made to treat malaria, yellow fever and sleeping sickness.

Did these new ideas have an impact on treatment of disease in Britain?

Robert Koch identified the bacillus that caused diphtheria in 1891. He produced a successful serum in 1894. Joseph Lister used this serum in Britain from 1895 and death rates plummeted. Within ten years the death rate from the disease had more than halved. From around 1880 onwards death rates from the traditional 'killer' diseases began to fall, especially in cities. But as we shall see in Topic 3.4 this might be as much to do with improvements in public health as in scientific medicine.

Infant mortality

Infant mortality, the number of babies that die before their first birthday, remained incredibly high in Britain. In 1899 it was 142 per thousand. In other words, 142 out of every thousand babies born died before their first birthday. In some areas it was higher still. In York, in 1899, it was 250 per thousand. Obviously poor families had higher death rates than richer ones, but why were the figures so high? Medicine was beginning to conquer infectious diseases like diphtheria, yet seemed unable to reduce infant mortality. Lots of reasons have been put forward to explain these figures, some more convincing than others. Many people could not afford doctors, so still relied on old 'tried and tested' family remedies. Many children were neglected, as both parents had to work to pay the rent and buy food. Babies were often left in the care of older people, or young children, while the parents were out at work. Bad housing and overcrowding meant disease spread quickly. Lack of fresh food – most people ate mainly bread and meat – meant it was hard to fight off illness.

> **THINK**
>
> 1 How had ideas about the cause of disease changed during the nineteenth century?
> 2 How important was science in bringing about these changes?
> 3 Find out what the infant mortality figure is in Britain today.
> 4 If older people were living longer (see page 5), why did infant mortality remain so high?

PROFILES

Louis Pasteur, 1822–95

- A French chemist, known as the 'father of microbiology'.
- He discovered germ theory – the idea that disease is spread by tiny organisms he called germs.
- He built on Jenner's work on vaccination, and learned how to 'grow' vaccines in the laboratory.
- He is perhaps most famous for his rabies vaccine.
- He invented the process of pasteurisation, named after him, to preserve liquids and stop them spoiling.

Robert Koch, 1843–1910

- A German microbiologist, Koch won a Nobel Prize in 1905.
- He invented a way to stain bacteria so it was easier to see them under the microscope.
- He and his team developed an experimental approach to discover which bacteria caused which disease, and thus identified the bacteria that causes anthrax, tuberculosis and cholera.

Paul Ehrlich, 1854–1915

- A German physician, Ehrlich initially worked for Koch.
- He won a Nobel Prize in 1908.
- He used staining techniques to study blood cells and then worked on immunity, developing an anti-diphtheria SERUM.
- His work on chemotherapy led to the idea of 'magic bullets' that would target specific organisms in the body. He developed Salvarsan as a treatment for syphilis.

How safe were you in hospital at this time?

Luke Fildes' painting, *The Doctor*, exhibited at the Royal Academy in 1891

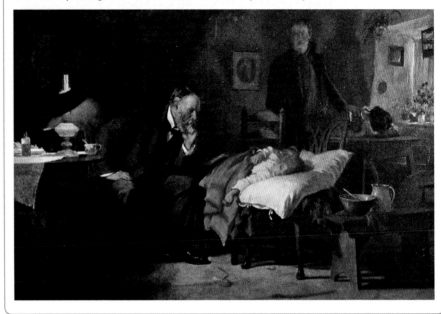

THINK

1 Look carefully at this popular Victorian painting (Source 1). Can you identify:
   a) the victim
   b) the parents
   c) the physician?
2 What tools is the physician using to help treat the child?
3 How useful is a painting like this as evidence of medicine in the nineteenth century?
4 Using this painting as evidence, how widespread do you think the scientific approach to treating disease in Britain was at this time?
5 What would it be like to be a patient in this hospital ward (Source 2)?
6 Does it look like there has been a revolution in science applied to this new hospital?
7 How similar, and how different, is this ward to the hospitals you studied in Topic 2.3 (page 41) and Topic 1.4 (page 20)?

Of course, the patient in Source 1 is being treated in their own home. Many people were treated in hospital. Hospitals were, as we have already seen (page 41), not renowned either for their surgeons or their nurses. That, too, changed throughout the nineteenth century. Many new hospitals were built, some by public subscription and some by large employers for their workers. By 1860 there were 36 specialist hospitals in London alone. In 1870, the London Hospital Saturday Fund was set up to collect donations from workmen and then arranged admission 'tickets' for treatment as and when necessary.

A ward in Great Ormond Street Hospital, built in 1875

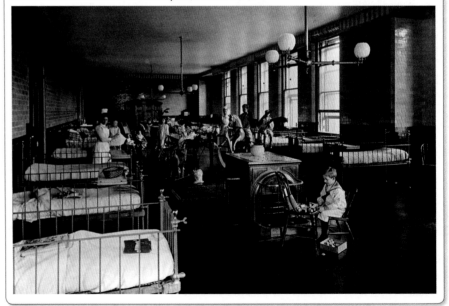

Florence Nightingale: A significant individual?

Everyone knows the story of Florence Nightingale and the Crimean War – how she cleaned up hospital wards and drastically cut mortality rates, from 40 per cent to just 2 per cent. Florence's family were totally opposed to her becoming a nurse as it was regarded as a very unsavoury occupation indeed! In fact she had to go to Germany to train. Returning to Britain after the Crimean War Florence wrote a book, *Notes on Nursing*, explaining her ideas on how nurses should be trained and how they should treat the sick. She set up Britain's first nurse training school at St Thomas' Hospital. She had to raise the £44,000 to fund it herself. She aimed to make nursing an honourable profession. *Notes on Hospitals* followed in 1863, setting out her principles for running clean, safe and well-ventilated hospitals.

Charles E. Rosenberg argues that Florence,

> 'was one of the few individuals who exerted a peculiar and indispensable influence … Her two most widely read books had an extraordinary success in the second half of the century; it would be hard to overestimate her influence in the shaping of modern nursing and the reordering of hospitals.'

(From *Explaining Epidemics and Other Studies in the History of Medicine*, Cambridge University Press, 1992)

Judith Cromwell argues that,

> 'Nightingale changed the concept of hospital nurse from drunken menial to medical professional. Yes, in the Crimean War she made her rounds at night carrying a lamp, and she ministered to thousands of sick and wounded soldiers. But she did much more than that. Starting with basic cleanliness, she was a genius at organising hospitals into model medical institutions.'

(From *Florence Nightingale, Feminist*, McFarland & Co. Inc., 2012)

SOURCE 3

The monument to Florence Nightingale in Waterloo Place, London

According to a recent book by Anne Summers, Nightingale's importance during the Crimean War has been exaggerated and her reputation is largely due to the propagandistic efforts of contemporary newspaper reporters. The recent argument that Mary Seacole, rather than Florence Nightingale, should be part of the History National Curriculum shows how emotive people feel about the subject.

ACTIVITY

How can we reach a conclusion about the significance of Florence Nightingale when she is regarded as an icon by most people, and an imposter by others? You could use the following criteria to help decide whether or not someone is significant:

If they:
- changed events at the time they lived
- improved lots of people's lives – or made them worse
- changed people's ideas
- had a long-lasting impact on their country or the world
- were a really good or a very bad example to other people of how to live or behave.

1   In pairs, discuss this criteria of significance. Do you agree with it? Would you add any other points?

2   Now decide upon your own criteria to judge the significance of Florence Nightingale.

Everyday medical treatments and remedies

THINK

Study Source 4.

1 What ailments does this medicine profess to cure?
2 How much did a bottle cost? At this time the average wage for a semi-skilled worker was £1 per week.
3 Is there a list of ingredients?
4 How do we know if it works?
5 Why do you think there was such a market for these products?
6 Why were there no controls over these products?
7 What do medicines of this type tell us about medical practice in the nineteenth century?

SOURCE 4

A commercial response to people's ailments, 1888

Technology helped the development of medicines. Machines were invented to make tablets, sugar-coated pills and even GELATIN CAPSULES. These allowed accurate doses of medicine to be taken, and the mass production of drugs. Mrs Beeton's famous self-help book for those running a household, *The Book of Household Management*, first published in 1861, and still in print today, recommended every household should have opium powders and laudanum in their medical cupboards in order to treat minor ailments. Laudanum, made from 90 per cent alcohol and 10 per cent opium, flavoured to give a pleasant taste, was a common Victorian cure. It was often given to children to calm them, send them to sleep, or to keep them quiet while mother worked (as many Victorian women worked at home).

The market was flooded with all kinds of medicines, some more effective than others. Aspirin, for example, was developed by a German chemical company in the 1890s, derived from a traditional remedy of willow bark, and went on sale in Britain in 1899 as an everyday painkiller. Many names that are common to us today, like Boots the Chemist, began in the nineteenth century, making patent medicines for the home market. Thomas Beecham (of Beecham's Powders fame) opened his first factory in Wigan in 1859.

There were no controls over the production of these medicines – anyone could include anything they wanted in them. Alcohol was a major ingredient in many. Some products, like aspirin, were (and still remain) effective; others were downright dangerous containing arsenic and mercury, both poisonous in large quantities. Others were addictive, with large amounts of cocaine and opium as their active ingredients. One thing is clear: there was a ready market for these treatments and people like Thomas Beecham rapidly became very rich selling them.

TOPIC SUMMARY

The development of germ theory
- Louis Pasteur and Robert Koch revolutionised the way people understood what caused disease.
- Paul Ehrlich changed the approach to treating disease when he discovered the first 'magic bullet'.
- The impact of some diseases was dramatically reduced, but other diseases remained deadly. Infant mortality remained very high.
- Nursing and hospitals were transformed by the work of, among others, Florence Nightingale.
- Many people still could not afford medical treatment. This led to a ready market for manufactured remedies.
- There was no control over the drug industry at this time.

PROGRESS CHECK

Significance

1 How significant was the work of Pasteur, Koch and Ehrlich in the understanding of the causes of disease and their treatment?

Now answer this question:

2 To what extent had science improved medicine for all by 1900?

3.3 A revolution in surgery

FOCUS

We have already seen that mortality rates from surgery were 40 per cent or higher. Partly this was because the process was so brutal that many died, but many more died from infection caught *after* their operation. Hospitals could still be dangerous places. Yet, by the end of the nineteenth century, mortality rates were often as low as 10 per cent. This topic explores the changes in the way operations were carried out and asks if there really was a revolution in surgery.

Becoming a surgeon

In 1828 a London surgeon, Bransby Blake Cooper, operated on a labourer to remove a stone from his bladder. This usually took six minutes, but Cooper took about an hour to operate. The patient died the next day. The *Lancet,* a medical journal, suggested Cooper had only been appointed to his post at Guy's Hospital because he was the nephew of a distinguished surgeon, and wasn't competent enough to keep his post. Surgeons were often appointed because they knew someone, rather than on the basis of how good they were! There was a libel trial which exposed the whole case to public scrutiny. This, and similar cases, led to the establishment of the General Medical Council in 1858 to regulate the profession.

Elizabeth Garrett Anderson

The medical profession was increasingly an all-male one. It was very difficult for women to get medical training or to be accepted as doctors. Elizabeth Garrett Anderson became one of the first, in 1865, but only after working as a surgery nurse and having private education (no university in Britain would accept her on a medical course) and passing an examination of the Society of Apothecaries to get a licence. She received the highest marks of all those taking the exam and the Society of Apothecaries immediately changed its rules to prevent other women from taking its examinations.

Unable to work in a hospital, Elizabeth set up her own practice, including an outpatients' service for the poor. This became the New Hospital for Women and Children in 1872, staffed entirely by women. In 1870 she learned French in order to obtain a medical degree from the Sorbonne in Paris (a medical school that did accept women). She gained membership of the British Medical Association in 1873, but was the only woman member for nearly twenty years. She helped set up the London School of Medicine for Women in 1874, which was the only teaching hospital in Britain to offer courses to women. By 1911 there were only 495 women on the Medical Register in Britain.

THINK

1 Why was it so difficult for Elizabeth Garrett Anderson to become a doctor?
2 Why do you think she set up the New Hospital for Women and Children?

Sophia Jex-Blake

Sophia Jex-Blake was another female medical pioneer. Born in 1840 she was educated at a series of private schools before enrolling in Queen's College, London in 1858. She was offered the post of mathematics tutor at the college in 1859 but her father only allowed her to take the post if she wasn't paid! No daughter of his was to work for a living. After visiting the USA (and trying to get admission to Harvard to study medicine) she was determined to become a doctor and in 1869 applied to Edinburgh University to study medicine. The university rejected her application, saying it could not make arrangements for just one female student so Sophia advertised in the Scottish newspapers for more students and eventually the 'Edinburgh Seven' were allowed to start the course.

SOURCE 1

Sophia Jex-Blake, the pioneering English female doctor

In 1870 what became known as the Surgeon's Hall riot took place. Male students rioted as the women went to take their anatomy examination, pelting them with mud and rubbish. This event was a turning point however, as some attitudes changed. Some male students escorted the women to lectures and examinations to prevent further indiscipline. The university staff was divided however, and refused to issue degrees. Jex-Blake had to attend the University of Berne, in Switzerland, to obtain her medical degree in 1877.

Jex-Blake became only the third female doctor in the country, and opened her own surgery in Edinburgh in 1878. She was involved with Elizabeth Garrett Anderson in opening the New Hospital for Women and Children in London, and in setting up a similar institution in Edinburgh.

Interestingly, Edinburgh University, having refused to issue a degree to Jex-Blake and the other members of the 'Edinburgh Seven', now proudly boasts of Sophia on its 'alumni' (graduate) page and has a plaque to her near the entrance to the Medical School praising her as 'Physician, pioneer of medical education for women in Britain, alumna of the University'.

THINK

1 Why do you think Jex-Blake's father was so adamant that she could not work for money? What does that tell us about the role of better-off women in Victorian society?
2 Why was it so difficult for Jex-Blake to become a doctor?
3 What are the similarities of Jex-Blake's story, with that of Garrett Anderson? What are the differences?
4 What do the experiences of Jex-Blake and Garrett Anderson tell us about the medical profession in the nineteenth century?
5 Why do you think Jex-Blake is now honoured as an alumna of Edinburgh University, even though the university refused to issue her degree?

What part did James Simpson play in making operations endurable?

As Fanny Burney's operation (page 37) shows, surgery was accompanied by pain. Many surgeons believed patients *should* experience pain, as it helped them appreciate the efforts being made on their behalf! Copious amounts of alcohol or opium were often used to try to subdue a patient and thus make an operation easier to perform. Sir Humphrey Davy, who invented the Miner's Safety Lamp in 1815, was one of the first to use nitrous oxide, or laughing gas as we know it. He invited his friends to inhale the gas from oiled silk bags. Quickly the gas was used

PROFILE

James Simpson, 1811–70

- A Scottish scientist, Simpson was famous for his work with anaesthetics during operations.
- He discovered that chloroform was effective, after trying it out on himself and friends.
- He was an obstetrician and improved the design of forceps used for delivering babies.

as an anaesthetic to relieve pain during operations, but it was difficult to control the dose. In 1846 Robert Liston successfully amputated a leg using ether as an anaesthetic, copying his ideas from an American dentist, William Morton. However, one drawback of this was that sometimes the patient woke up in the middle of the operation!

SOURCE 2
Administering anaesthetic

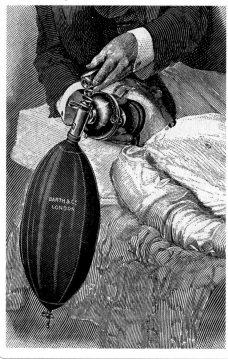

SOURCE 3
A replica of the first successful ether inhaler, devised by William Morton in 1846 and used in an operation to remove a tumour from the neck of a patient

In 1847 James Simpson used chloroform after experimenting on himself and his friends, to reduce pain in childbirth. Chloroform induces dizziness, sleepiness and unconsciousness in patients, and needs to be carefully administered. Not surprisingly there was opposition in many quarters to the use of these painkillers, but this was partly overcome in 1853 when Queen Victoria used chloroform while having a baby. If it was good enough for the Queen then it was good enough for anybody! All these painkillers had to be inhaled as a general anaesthetic in order to work. Finally, in the 1850s, coca leaves from South America were used to produce cocaine that could be used as a local anaesthetic, on the first occasion as drops in the eye. The use of cocaine rapidly spread, especially once it could be produced chemically after 1891. By the end of the century operations no longer had to be painful!

Anaesthetics did not necessarily make operations safer. It was difficult to get the dose right with early painkillers. Also, surgeons tried more difficult operations because they could take longer to operate. But unfortunately, there was still no control over infection. Some surgeons had higher mortality rates using anaesthetics than before, so in the 1870s some stopped using chloroform altogether.

THINK

6 Why was pain seen to be a 'good thing' by surgeons?
7 What part did science play in developing effective anaesthetics?
8 Why was it so difficult to get the dose right in early anaesthetics?
9 Humphrey Davy used nitrous oxide as a 'recreational drug', so why did the British Government take steps in July 2015 to ban the sale of nitrous oxide?

Beating infection: Joseph Lister and carbolic acid

If we cut or graze ourselves today the first thing we do is wash the cut, then apply some antiseptic cream, or a plaster. The idea is to prevent dirt getting into the wound, and to prevent infection. It is widely known that dirt can kill. But all this is relatively recent. The biggest killer after surgery was sepsis infection, otherwise known as hospital gangrene, an infection caught during or after an operation. We have already seen the opposition from surgeons to the idea that they themselves spread infection, in the work of Alexander Gordon (page 46).

Ignaz Semmelweiss was the pioneer in antiseptics in 1847. He was in charge of the maternity ward at Vienna General Hospital in Austria. He dramatically reduced the death rate on his ward from around 35 per cent to less than 1 per cent by insisting that doctors wash their hands in calcium chloride solution before treating their patients. Despite publishing his results, very few other hospitals introduced the procedure.

Joseph Lister

After Pasteur published his germ theory (page 54), Joseph Lister used an operating room sterilised with carbolic acid. He based his ideas on experiments he carried out on frogs. As cold-blooded mammals, he could observe more clearly the impact of the changes he was introducing. His surgical instruments were sterilised with carbolic acid, too. He also soaked the wound from time to time with carbolic acid, and used dressings sterilised in exactly the same way. By doing this he managed to reduce the mortality rate in his operations from 46 per cent to 15 per cent in only three years. In 1871 he invented a machine that sprayed carbolic acid over the entire room, surgeon, patient, assistants, everything! Others copied his methods and Lister became known as the 'father of antiseptic surgery'.

THINK

1 Do you think Joseph Lister should have a statue in Parliament Square to commemmorate him?

SOURCE 4

An operation in progress using Lister's carbolic spray, 1880s

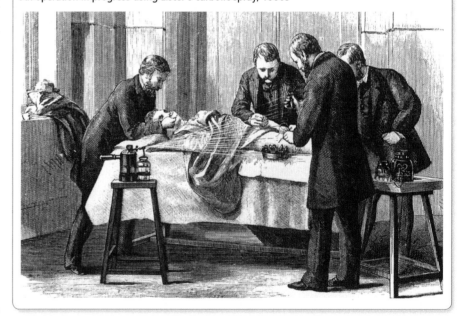

Aseptic surgery: A real change at last?

Further improvements were made later in the century with the development of ASEPTIC surgery. This followed on from the work of Robert Koch (pages 54–55), who discovered in 1878 that most disease was spread not by air but by contact with an infected surface. This led to attempts to create a germ-free environment in which to carry out operations as a way of avoiding spreading infection. In 1881 Charles Chamberland, a French biologist, invented a steam steriliser for medical instruments. He discovered that heating instruments in water at 140°C for 20 minutes completely sterilised them, making surgery much safer. This was the start of developing much simpler, less ornate and easier to sterilise tools for operations. As you might expect, few surgeons initially adopted this! The next step was by Gustav Neuber, a German surgeon in Kiel, who is recognised as having the first STERILE operating theatre. He insisted on thorough scrubbing before staff entered the theatre, even the air in the room was sterilised before they entered. He published a paper on the process and his results in 1886 and this quickly set the standard for others to follow.

Surgical clothing

The final part of the battle against infection was the (very gradual) adoption of protective clothing. William Halsted in America started his team wearing surgical gloves because one of the nurses developed an allergic reaction on her hand to the carbolic spray they were using. He asked the Goodyear Rubber Company to make special thin rubber gloves for her to use. Berkeley Moyniham, a respected British surgeon working in Leeds, became the first in Britain to wear gloves for an operation, and later made a point of always changing his clothes for surgical gowns before entering an operating theatre. He was regarded by most surgeons as an oddity for doing so! In fact, on one occasion his wife was presented with a bouquet made out of old rubber gloves!

What was the impact of all these changes?

There is no doubt that by the end of the century surgery was much safer than at the start. Anaesthetics allowed surgeons to carry out *careful* surgery, without the great need for speed. Antiseptic and then aseptic surgery massively reduced the risk of infection during and after surgery. There wasn't a revolution in surgery in the sense of innovative operations, but there was a revolution in the chances of the patient surviving surgery. However, for a whole variety of reasons, there was opposition to these changes from the establishment. Some were jealous of Simpson and Lister; some were worried by the inaccuracies of carbolic acid; some simply thought they knew best, while others opposed change. There is clear evidence that in some cases mortality rates increased during antiseptic surgery. One famous British military surgeon argued during the Crimean War that it was better for soldiers in the hospital to hear the patient shout and bawl during an operation than to quietly subside and die!

TOPIC SUMMARY

A revolution in surgery

- Over 40 per cent of patients died as a result of operations.
- The surgical profession was predominantly male-only.
- James Simpson developed the first effective anaesthetic, making surgery safer.
- As Queen Victoria used chloroform to aid the delivery of her baby this technique became more popular.
- Joseph Lister developed the use of antiseptics in preventing hospital gangrene.
- Aseptic sterile surgery made a huge difference to survival rates.
- Many surgeons opposed these changes. In some hospitals change was slow to happen.

SOURCE 5

Berkeley Moyniham recalls his days as a student in Leeds in the 1880s. From *The Greatest Benefit to Mankind* by Roy Porter (Fontana Press, 1999), p.373

The surgeon arrived and threw off his jacket to avoid getting blood or pus on it. He rolled up his shirt sleeves and, in the corridor to the operation room, took an ancient frock from a cupboard; it bore signs of a chequered past, and was utterly stiff with old blood. One of these coats was worn with special pride, indeed joy, as it had belonged to a retired member of staff. The cuffs were rolled up to only just above the wrists, and the hands were washed in a sink. Once clean they were rinsed in carbolic-acid solution.

THINK

2 What is the difference between antiseptic surgery and aseptic surgery?

3 Which in your opinion had the greater impact?

4 How had these new methods altered the approach of the surgeon training students at Leeds in the 1880s (see Source 5)?

PROGRESS CHECK

Usefulness of sources

1 How useful is Source 3 in explaining the reason why survival rates after surgery were so much higher in this period?

Similarities and differences

2 Compare Source 4 with Source 2 in Chapter 2 on page 36. What similarities and differences are there in these two images of surgery?

Causes and consequences

3 To what extent had science improved surgery by 1900?

3.4 Improvements in public health

Medical moments in time: London, 1848

SOURCE 1

Population of Great Britain and Ireland, 1801–1901. From *Whitaker's Almanac*, 1941

Year	Population
1801	16.3m
1811	18.5m
1821	20.9m
1831	24.1m
1841	26.8m
1851	27.5m
1861	29.1m
1871	31.7m
1881	35.1m
1891	37.8m
1901	41.6m

Put honey on it. Mother said honey heals cuts and scrapes.

Hush, Victoria, it's only a graze. I'll bandage it with dropwort and comfrey.

Only the wealthy had homes with toilets and piped water. Most people shared outside toilets and got their water from a street pump.

Nonsense. If God meant surgery to be painless he would have made it painless.

Simpson says chloroform is an even better anaesthetic.

And that is how you amputate a leg using ether as an anaesthetic. The patient doesn't feel a thing.

Vaccination saves many children from smallpox. Dr Jenner was the greatest hero in medicine. I do hope science and experiments give us vaccinations against other diseases.

Roll up! Roll up! Buy the great 'Cure-all tonic'. Two spoonfuls will save you from cholera.

ACTIVITY

1 Look carefully at the picture. Can you identify:
   a) things that might be a public health hazard
   b) examples of the old ways of treating illnesses
   c) examples of medical progress?
2 Compare this picture of London in 1848 with the pictures of London in 1665 (pages 38–39) and 1347 (pages 22–23). Copy and complete the following table to show evidence of continuity and of change in medicine over this period.

Evidence of continuity in medicine, 1347–1848	Evidence of change in medicine, 1347–1848

3 Write a paragraph to summarise the progress in health in Victorian London.

50,000 people dead from cholera. It's worse than 1832.

It's this miasma of bad air that's causing it. People need clean air.

Hold your arm out. Bleeding does you good. And I've got a good laxative that'll clear out your whole body.

Toilets and cesspits were cleaned out by night-soil men and the waste was carried through streets on carts.

It's consumption. He's been coughing all week.

Back home, people with coughs ride a donkey in a circle seven times. Worth trying?

There's talk of taxes to pay for cleaning streets and building sewers and water pipes.

I'll pay for where I live but not for keeping anyone else clean.

Were the new industrial towns really that bad to live in?

The Victorians were exceptional at collecting data, and this is a great help in trying to discover what life was like in industrial towns. For example, we know that in Bethnal Green in east London, in 1842 richer people lived on average to the age of 45, whereas labourers lived until they were just 16. In Manchester at the same time 57 per cent of all children died before they reached their fifth birthday. Social surveys from the time show that often a whole family lived in one room, or in a cellar liable to flooding; many children shared a bed, and toilets and water pumps were shared by many families. There are plenty of other statistics we could use but these examples tell us that yes, indeed, the new industrial towns were grim to live in.

New hazards in industrial life

Added to the overcrowding were the new industrial diseases. Young boys forced to climb up chimneys came into contact with soot and gases. Percivall Pott, an English surgeon, identified SCROTAL CANCER in many of these chimney boys. Young girls making matches at factories across London developed 'phossy-jaw' caused by the fumes from the phosphorous used to make the match heads. Parts of the jaw would be eaten away, or glow greenish-white in the dark. It also caused brain damage. Coal miners developed pneumoconiosis, a disease of the lungs, caused by inhaling dust below ground. Machines in the new textile factories rarely had guards, and hands and arms were often caught in the machines. There were few regulations controlling working conditions and accidents were common, with no compensation and little prospect of further work.

There were no regulations about food either. Bakers added powdered chalk to flour in order to make more money. Dairies watered down milk then added chalk powder to make it white again. Adam Hart-Davis, in his book *What the Victorians Did For Us*, cites the example of William Luby, who saw his employer making chocolate by mixing brown paint with melted candle wax before selling it to children; he also saw him buying sugar sweepings from the floor of a grocer's shop and boiling them down to make toffee!

THINK

Study Source 2.

1 Try to imagine what it would be like living in one of these houses. How do you keep clean and tidy? Where do you get your water from? Where do you go to the toilet? How likely is your washing to dry or to stay clean? What would happen if your neighbour fell ill?

2 To what extent does Doré's engraving agree with the other evidence we have from Victorian times about life in the new towns?

SOURCE 2

An engraving by Gustave Doré of part of London in 1872

In 1858 it was proposed that Parliament should leave London because of the 'Great Stink'. Exceptionally dry weather had combined with a build-up of EFFLUENT, both human and industrial, because there had been no rain to wash it all into the River Thames. In *Little Dorrit*, published in instalments between 1855 and 1857, Charles Dickens wrote that the Thames was a 'deadly sewer … in the place of a fine, fresh river'. The Great Stink was particularly threatening because at the time the 'miasma theory' of disease (see page 44) was still most widely believed.

Contagious disease was no respecter of rank. In 1861 Prince Albert died, probably of typhoid, caught from the sewers at Windsor Castle. Contagious diseases like typhoid, typhus, diarrhoea, smallpox, tuberculosis, scarlet fever, whooping cough, measles and chickenpox all spread rapidly in poor and overcrowded conditions. No wonder 57 per cent of children died before they reached the age of five. Perhaps the best indicator of how bad conditions were is the prevalence of rickets, known in the nineteenth century as 'the English Disease'. This was a crippling bone disease common in infants, caused by calcium deficiency and lack of fresh air and sunlight, and was a clear indicator of malnutrition. In Paris in 1907 it was found that 50 per cent of children between the ages of six months and three years suffered from rickets.

Here comes the cholera

Perhaps the biggest agent for change at this time were the cholera epidemics of 1831–32, 1848, 1854 and 1866. Cholera originated in Bengal, and slowly spread along the trade routes, much like the Black Death in 1347. People knew it was coming, but hoped it would not arrive. At the time no one knew what caused cholera, or how to cure it.

John Snow and the discovery of the causes of cholera

John Snow had a surgery in Broad Street, London. In 1849, after the 1848 epidemic, he published a book arguing that cholera was spread by dirty water rather than through the air. Medical opinion pooh-poohed the idea and ignored his findings. In the first ten days of the cholera outbreak in 1854 over 700 people died in his locality. Snow carefully mapped the location of each death and worked out that the one thing they had in common was that they had all collected their water from the pump in Broad Street. He also noticed that men in a nearby brewery, who drank beer rather than water, had not been victims of cholera. He obtained permission to remove the pump handle, forcing people to collect water elsewhere. Immediately the disease abated in Broad Street. It was later discovered that a cess pit, less than one metre from the water pump, was leaking dirty water into the water supply. Careful scientific investigation had helped to find the cause of cholera, long before Pasteur and his germ theory was published.

SOURCE 3

UK deaths from cholera

1831–32	50,000
1848	60,000
1854	20,000

SOURCE 4

Notice issued in Limehouse in 1866 giving advice for dealing with cholera

BOARD OF WORKS
FOR THE LIMEHOUSE DISTRICT.
COMPRISING LIMEHOUSE, RATCLIFF, SHADWELL & WAPPING.

In consequence of the appearance of **CHOLERA** within this District, the Board have appointed the under-mentioned Medical Gentlemen who will give **ADVICE, MEDICINE, AND ASSISTANCE, FREE OF ANY CHARGE, AND UPON APPLICATION, AT ANY HOUR OF THE DAY OR NIGHT.**

The Inhabitants are earnestly requested not to neglect the first symptoms of the appearance of Disease, (which in its early stage is easy to cure), but to apply, **WITHOUT DELAY**, to one of the Medical Gentlemen appointed.

The Board have opened an Establishment for the reception of Patients, in a building at Green Bank, near Wapping Church, (formerly used as Wapping Workhouse), where all cases of Cholera and Diarrhoea will be received and placed under the care of a competent Resident Medical Practitioner, and proper Attendants.

THE FOLLOWING ARE THE MEDICAL GENTLEMEN TO BE APPLIED TO:--

Mr. ORTON,
56, White Horse Street.

Dr. NIGHTINGALL,
4, Commercial Terrace, Commercial Road, (near Limehouse Church.)

Mr. SCHROEDER,
53, Three Colt Street, Limehouse.

Mr. HARRIS,
5, York Terrace, Commercial Road, (opposite Stepney Railway Station.)

Mr. CAMBELL,
At Mr. GRAY's, Chemist, Old Road, opposite "The World's End."

Mr. LYNCH,
St. James's Terrace, Back Road, Shadwell.

Mr. HECKFORD,
At the Dispensary, Wapping Workhouse.

By Order,
THOS. W. RATCLIFF,
Clerk to the Board.

BOARD OFFICES, White Horse Street,
26th July, 1866.

THINK

3 Study Source 4. What advice does it give to people who think they have cholera?

4 Given the state of knowledge about cholera at the time, how effective is this advice?

5 How does this compare to the advice given about treating the Black Death (page 27) and the Plague (page 47)?

6 How does this advice compare with contemporary ideas about the spread of disease?

Laissez-faire

Variously translated as 'do nothing', or 'it's not my place to do this'. This was the attitude held by the governments of the day. It is important to realise this was not a callous indifference. It was a genuinely held belief that such problems were not the concern of government. It was up to individuals to sort these things out for themselves.

Poor Laws

There have been Poor Laws in England since Tudor times, when each parish was made responsible for looking after its poor. In 1834 the Poor Law Amendment Act was passed, setting up workhouses. If you wanted poor relief (or help) you had to go into the workhouse to get it. Poor people hated workhouses, calling them 'Bastilles' after the French prison. Commissioners were set up to run the system and to ensure life inside a workhouse was worse than outside, to act as a deterrent. Charles Dickens' Oliver Twist famously asks for 'more' food in a workhouse.

1 What part did Farr, Southwood Smith, and Chadwick play in improving public health in the nineteenth century?
2 In what way were the actions of Thomas Barnardo different to the other reformers mentioned here?
3 Why was the debate over reform referred to as the 'Clean Party versus the Dirty Party'?

Agents of change

In 1854 a letter to *The Times* newspaper stated, 'We prefer to take our chance with cholera rather than be bullied into health'. This epitomises the great struggle that took place in the nineteenth century to persuade the Government to act over living and working conditions. The prevailing attitude was known as *laissez-faire*.

Farr and Southwood Smith

William Farr, a civil servant, was the driving force behind the compulsory registration of births, marriages and deaths in 1837. Up until then churches had kept records but in an increasingly SECULAR society Farr realised the power of numbers as well as the need for accurate information. Thomas Southwood Smith was another influential figure. In 1824 he was appointed physician to the London Fever Hospital. This allowed him to study the diseases caused by poverty. The papers he published on public health provided examples and data to support the work of Edwin Chadwick, perhaps the most influential reformer of the 1830s and 1840s.

Chadwick

Edwin Chadwick was Secretary to the Poor Law Commissioners from 1834, and he used statistical methods of investigation to explore the link between ill-health and poverty. He was the author of the influential 1842 *Report on the Sanitary Conditions of the Labouring Population*, which established the link between poor living conditions, disease and life expectancy. The report argued that there was an urgent need to improve living conditions if the economy was to continue to grow. He, along with Southwood Smith, was the driving force behind the Health of Towns Association set up in 1844 and part of what became known as the 'Clean Party'. The Clean Party were those pushing for government action to improve conditions in towns. The 'Dirty Party' as they became known were those MPs and others opposed to any such action. Their opposition was largely based on the monumental costs involved. Ratepayers, the wealthier people in a town, were keen to keep their rates (local taxes used to pay for local government) as low as possible so they favoured inaction!

Dr Barnardo and the Ragged School

Thomas Barnardo came to London in 1866 to train as a doctor. He was appalled by the poverty he found in the East End. In response, he set up a 'Ragged School', a place where hungry children were given a cheap breakfast to help them learn better. In times of great unemployment meals were served too. There were evening classes and Sunday Schools for those in work. There was a Wood-Chopping Brigade, and a City Messenger's Brigade to help boys find work once they left school, and there was a Factory Girls' Club and Institute to support girls. At school they were taught the skills needed to be maids or servants, and the school helped them find work in this area, or in the local factories like Bryant & May's match factory, or Tate and Lyle's sugar refinery. Barnardo also opened a series of homes for children, with the slogan, 'No DESTITUTE child ever turned away'. There was a 'Fresh Air Fund' and a 'Children's Country Holiday Fund' to provide an opportunity to get out into the countryside occasionally. There were also schemes to send boys to Canada and Australia as farm workers after being trained in England. The aim was to give them a better life than they would have as destitute children in London.

SOURCE 5

Two children rescued from a slum in London in 1908 and taken to a Barnardo's home

The Government acts at last: The great clean-up

It was the cholera epidemic of 1848 rather than the Health of Towns Association that finally forced the Government to act. It passed the 1848 Public Health Act. This allowed local councils to improve conditions in their own town *if* they wished, and if they were prepared to pay for it. They could force towns with a particularly high death rate to take action over water supply and sewage, and appoint a Medical Officer of Health.

It was a start, but by 1872 only 50 councils had a Medical Officer of Health. Some towns, like Leeds, took steps to improve their facilities, but many did not. Other Acts followed, like the 1866 Sanitary Act, the 1875 Housing Act and finally the 1875 Public Health Act, which was the real breakthrough. This Act had more power. Local Councils were *forced* to provide clean water, and appoint Medical Officers of Health and Sanitary Inspectors. The 1875 Food and Drugs Act even regulated food and medicines. The great clean-up was under way and it was a success. In 1868 there were 716 deaths from typhus in London, in 1885 just 28 and by 1900 there were none.

London started building new sewers in 1858, and without doubt new sewers improved living conditions and public health. But there were other contributing factors. The 1875 Housing Act allowed councils to knock down bad housing and replace it. Flush toilets became more widely used in better-off homes and new products, like Pear's Soap, became available cheaply, making it easier for people and clothes to stay clean. And don't forget, compulsory vaccination against smallpox was introduced in 1853 (see page 45).

FACTFILES

1848 Public Health Act

This Act created the Central Board of Health. Although the Board was abolished ten years later, the Act also encouraged local Boards of Health to be set up to appoint a Medical Officer, provide sewers, inspect lodging houses and check food which was offered for sale.

1875 Public Health Act

This brought together a range of Acts covering sewerage and drains, water supply, housing and disease. Local authorities had to appoint Medical Officers in charge of public health. Local sanitary inspectors were appointed to look after slaughterhouses and prevent contaminated food being sold. Local authorities were ordered to cover sewers, keep them in good condition, supply fresh water to their citizens, collect rubbish and provide street lighting.

TOPIC SUMMARY

Improvements in public health

- The Industrial Revolution led to the rapid growth of towns, and the spread of unsanitary living conditions.
- Diseases spread rapidly in such conditions.
- Governments were reluctant to act.
- Many individuals played a key part in changing attitudes to public health.
- Cholera finally persuaded the Government to pass a Public Health Act.
- By 1900 conditions in the industrial towns were improving.

PROGRESS CHECK

Significance

1 How significant is John Snow's discovery of the causes of cholera in improving public health?
2 What was the significance of the 1875 Public Health Act?

Causes and factors

3 To what extent had public health improved by 1900, and how much of this was down to actions by the Government?

Now answer this question:

4 Why did the Government change its attitude to intervening in public health during the nineteenth century?

3.5 Pulling it all together:
Nineteenth-century Britain

A case study of Lincoln in 1905

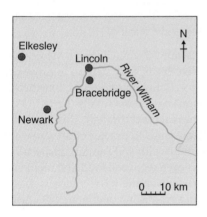

In late December 1904 an outbreak of typhoid occurred in the city of Lincoln. In the next few months over 130 people died as the epidemic raged across the city. The new isolation hospital was quickly overwhelmed with cases, and meeting places and the local Drill Hall were taken over as emergency hospitals. This case study explores the cause of the epidemic, and asks what it tells us about progress in medicine throughout the nineteenth century.

> **SOURCE 1**
>
> Advert in the *Lincolnshire Chronicle*, 3 February 1905
>
> CITY OF LINCOLN.
> TYPHOID FEVER.
> During the existence of the present outbreak of Typhoid Fever in the City the Inhabitants are particularly urged, as a matter of precaution, not to consume either WATER or MILK until the same has been THOROUGHLY BOILED.
> By Order of the Health Committee.
> W. T. PAGE, JR.,
> Deputy Town Clerk and Clerk to the Urban Sanitary Authority.
> Lincoln, Jan. 27th, 1905.

Lincoln, like most cities, had grown rapidly towards the end of the nineteenth century. By 1901 it had over 50,000 inhabitants; many working in the new engineering works. Rustons, the biggest employer, had over 5,000 workers and made and exported agricultural machinery and railway equipment across the world. The City had a Friday market, a butter market and a weekly cattle market. Each April there was a sheep fair, and the horse fair was the biggest in the country. Lincoln Racecourse was well-known and a popular place to watch the Races.

In 1871 Lincoln Corporation had taken over the waterworks, followed by the sewerage company, the gas company and even the electric company. It opened the first public library in 1889, and a horse tramway in 1897. To all appearances it looked like a modern, go-ahead council. Yet the councillors and aldermen, those running the council, wanted it all on the cheap. Rates were kept low, and expenses at a minimum. New sewers had been completed in 1881, but only after the Government in London had insisted the council build them. There had been a smallpox epidemic in 1893 and 'bad water' was blamed for that, yet no efforts had been made to improve either the environs of the town or the quality of the drinking water.

> More than 300,000 households in Lancashire have been told to boil drinking water after contamination with a microbial parasite. Traces were found in recent samples of water from Franklaw water treatment plant.
>
> (From the BBC News website, 7 August 2015)

THINK

1. Why were the residents of Lancashire advised to boil their drinking water in 2015 (see above)?
2. Why were the residents of Lincoln advised to boil their drinking water in 1905 (see Source 1)?
3. What post did W. T. Page hold?
4. What does this tell us about Lincoln and public health?

> **SOURCE 2**
>
> The Drill Hall, Lincoln in use as an emergency hospital ward

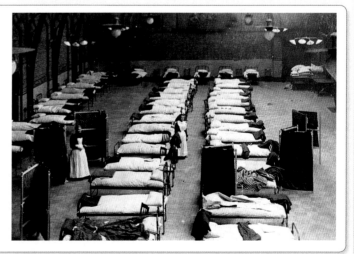

Lincoln obtained its water from the River Witham, from local streams and from disused gravel pits. There were some local springs, and some houses had their own well; there was even a medieval conduit (channel) installed by monks still delivering water outside St Mary-le-Wigford Church on the High Street. But the rapidly increasing population was putting great strain on the water supply. The Medical Officer of Health drew the Council's attention to the poor quality of the water in 1879, and there were continuing disputes about its quality. It was known that raw sewage entered the River Witham 30 miles upstream of Lincoln, but the Council considered this would be suitably dissipated before the water reached Lincoln and was extracted for human use. It was openly admitted that Lincoln had 'second-rate, but acceptable water'.

On 2 January 1905, the Medical Officer of Health reported an outbreak of typhoid. By 4 February, 408 cases had been reported, with 23 deaths. The Sanitary Inspector himself died on 17 February. By 23 February, 732 cases had been reported with 61 deaths. Many cases were being treated at home, or in emergency hospital wards like the Drill Hall. An appeal was issued for horse blankets to cover the sick.

From 17 February, railway companies were bringing water by train from nearby Newark, and the council street-watering carts were being used to bring cleaner water from nearby towns and deliver it around the city. In March, the Council ordered a clean-up of the city, ordering overflowing privies to be emptied, and cats and dogs, chickens and pigs removed from gardens and the streets. Many poor people at the time belonged to a 'pig club', keeping a pig at the bottom of the garden and slaughtering it in the autumn.

By March, most of the victims were either young or old, with 931 cases and 102 deaths. Of these cases, over 500 had to be treated at home because there was nowhere else for them to go. By the end of April, over 1,000 cases had been confirmed before the epidemic began to subside. Many workers contributed subscriptions to the Distress Fund set up to help those who could no longer work or look after themselves. In June, the Bishop of Lincoln preached a sermon of thanksgiving, claiming that the outbreak had been 'the hand of God'.

Facing severe criticism from the people of Lincoln, as early as March 1905 the Council met to try to identify new sources of water. The Waterworks Engineer resigned and left the town. Finally the Council agreed to pump in water from Elkesley, in Nottinghamshire, at a cost of over £200,000. A Private Act of Parliament was passed in 1908. (It was opposed by many in Nottinghamshire who accused Lincoln of 'stealing their water'.) It took three years for the work to be completed, but by October 1911 there was a brand new reservoir at nearby Bracebridge, a new pumping station at Elkesley, and a new water main bringing clean water to the city.

SOURCE 3

Advert in the *Lincolnshire Chronicle*, 18 February 1905

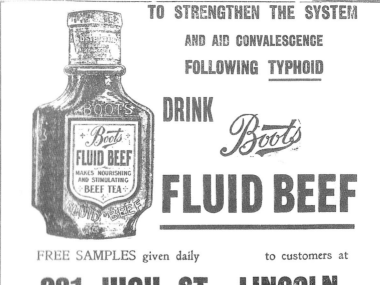

TO STRENGTHEN THE SYSTEM AND AID CONVALESCENCE FOLLOWING TYPHOID

DRINK *Boots* FLUID BEEF

BOOTS FLUID BEEF MAKES NOURISHING AND STIMULATING BEEF TEA

FREE SAMPLES given daily to customers at

281 HIGH ST., LINCOLN.

THINK

5   What appears to be the cause of the typhoid epidemic in 1905?

6   How did the Council try to control the outbreak?

7   Who did the Bishop of Lincoln blame for the epidemic?

8   How is the response to the typhoid epidemic in Lincoln similar to, and how is it different from, the Black Death in 1347 (pages 26–27) and the Plague in 1665 (pages 47–48)?

Were people healthier in 1900?

By 1900 people had more choice over the type of treatment they received for disease than ever before. There were physicians, surgeons, apothecaries, and lots of off-the-peg commercial medicines. People could be treated at home or in hospital. They might be vaccinated and certainly the Government was now regulating both medical practitioners and medicines, as well as attempting to improve living conditions in the industrial towns and cities. Yet, as we have seen, in some towns nearly 90 per cent of men who volunteered to fight at the outbreak of the Boer War were rejected as unfit to serve, even by the low standards of the British Army.

FOCUS TASK

What happened to you if you fell ill in nineteenth-century Britain?

Now it's time to review your work on healthcare in nineteenth-century Britain. Below in the left-hand column you will find a list of ailments common in Victorian times. All you have to do is decide how those ailments would be treated, by whom and what the likely outcomes might be.

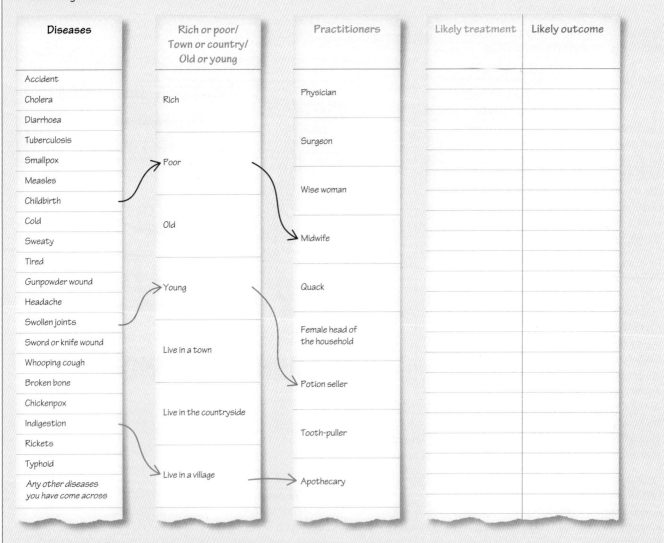

Diseases	Rich or poor/ Town or country/ Old or young	Practitioners	Likely treatment	Likely outcome
Accident				
Cholera	Rich	Physician		
Diarrhoea				
Tuberculosis		Surgeon		
Smallpox	Poor			
Measles		Wise woman		
Childbirth				
Cold	Old			
Sweaty		Midwife		
Tired				
Gunpowder wound	Young	Quack		
Headache				
Swollen joints		Female head of the household		
Sword or knife wound	Live in a town			
Whooping cough				
Broken bone		Potion seller		
Chickenpox				
Indigestion	Live in the countryside	Tooth-puller		
Rickets				
Typhoid				
Any other diseases you have come across	Live in a village	Apothecary		

1 Were some diseases more deadly than others?
2 Were some diseases easier to control than previously?
3 Was medical treatment, in your opinion, any better in 1900 than it had been in 1800? Or in 1600? Or in 1000?

Which factors inhibited or encouraged medical change at this time?

The title of this chapter is 'A revolution in medicine'. In it you have studied changing ideas about the cause of disease, the different ways of treating disease, improvements in surgery, and finally the way both government and individuals responded to the challenges of the Industrial Revolution. But does that add up, in your opinion, to a revolution in medicine? Are the changes significant enough to make people live longer and healthier lives? Could everyone get access to treatment, or was it only the rich? Have some previously deadly diseases disappeared, conquered by the changes? Or is life still, for most people, 'nasty, brutish and short'?

FOCUS TASK

Nineteenth-century Britain factor card

Throughout your course you will be thinking about how the following factors affected the story of Health and the People. Which of these factors were significant during the nineteenth century? We think at this time that the role of the individual is perhaps the most significant factor for change, and there are several to choose from: Pasteur, Koch, Ehrlich, Simpson, Lister, perhaps even Edwin Chadwick. Do you agree?

NINETEENTH-CENTURY BRITAIN		
Factor	Relative importance of the factor	Positive or negative influence
War		
Superstition and religion		
Chance		
Government		
Communication		
Science and technology		
The economy		
Ideas		
Role of the individual	5	+

1. On your own copy of the factor card decide which factors you think are most important in explaining any changes in health that took place during the nineteenth century. Give each factor a number value, where 1 is least important, and 5 most important. Remember to decide whether they are important for creating change, or for inhibiting change. In some cases, it might be both. You need to be able to explain *why* you think some factors were more important than others.
2. Discuss your findings in groups. Do other people in your group agree with your ideas?

KEY WORDS

Make sure you know what these words mean, and are able to use them confidently in your own writing. See the Glossary on pages 111–112 for definitions.
- Anaesthetic
- Aseptic
- Bacillus
- Serum
- Sterile

Modern medicine

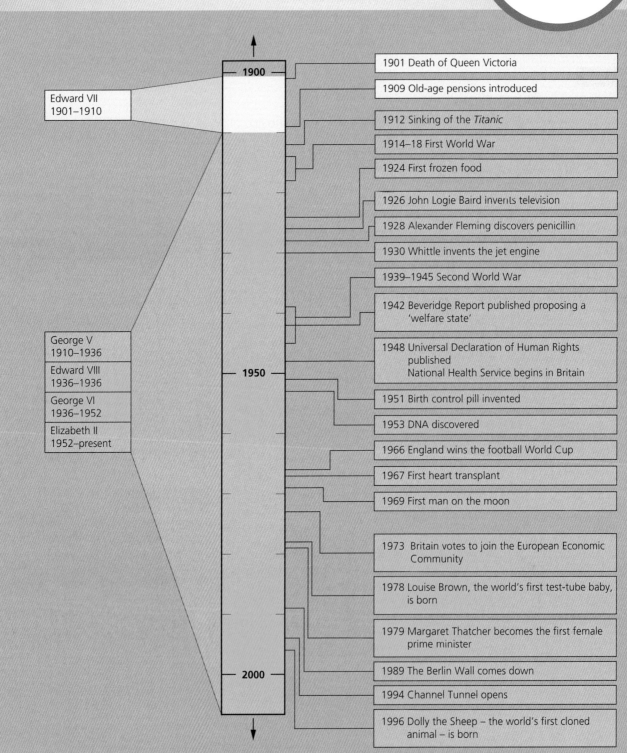

Edward VII
1901–1910

1900

1901 Death of Queen Victoria

1909 Old-age pensions introduced

1912 Sinking of the *Titanic*

1914–18 First World War

1924 First frozen food

1926 John Logie Baird invents television

1928 Alexander Fleming discovers penicillin

1930 Whittle invents the jet engine

1939–1945 Second World War

1942 Beveridge Report published proposing a 'welfare state'

1948 Universal Declaration of Human Rights published
National Health Service begins in Britain

George V
1910–1936

Edward VIII
1936–1936

George VI
1936–1952

Elizabeth II
1952–present

1950

1951 Birth control pill invented

1953 DNA discovered

1966 England wins the football World Cup

1967 First heart transplant

1969 First man on the moon

1973 Britain votes to join the European Economic Community

1978 Louise Brown, the world's first test-tube baby, is born

1979 Margaret Thatcher becomes the first female prime minister

2000

1989 The Berlin Wall comes down

1994 Channel Tunnel opens

1996 Dolly the Sheep – the world's first cloned animal – is born

4.1 Context: Twentieth-century Britain

THINK

You have probably studied twentieth-century Britain before. You may be quite an expert already.
So what do you think of our visual summary of this period? Discuss these questions.

1 Do you agree with the images we have chosen to summarise twentieth-century Britain?
  What do you think we have left out?
2 Which images would you use to sum up life in Britain at this time? Why?
3 How much change do you think there was between 1900 and 2000?
4 Are people better off today than they were in 1900?
5 What impact do you think these changes will have had on people's health?

'You've never had it so good!'

Perhaps the most telling illustration of Edwardian Britain is the *Titanic*, the 'unsinkable' ship that set sail from Southampton on 10 April 1912. Carrying 2,224 passengers and crew, the ship had lifeboats for about half that number. In the early hours of 12 April, the *Titanic* hit an iceberg and quickly sank; 1,513 people were lost. The figures for those saved make interesting reading (see Source 1).

The Liberal Government of 1906 introduced old-age pensions, at five shillings a week for those over 70. Perhaps it is war that has moulded society more than anything else throughout the twentieth century. Conscription sent men off to fight and women to work in occupations from which they had previously been excluded. Each played a vital part in securing victory for Britain in both world wars. Lloyd George won the 1918 election promising 'a land fit for heroes', and Labour won the 1945 election with a manifesto pledging the establishment of the WELFARE STATE and NATIONALISATION of the main industries. The National Health Service was introduced after the war in an attempt to provide people with free medical care 'from the cradle to the grave'.

There were great economic changes, too. Maud Pember Reeves wrote in 1913 of the respectable working class trying to get by on wages of £1 per week. Between the wars mass unemployment caused great hardship and the dreaded 'means test' provoked bitter resentment. New industries like motor cars and washing machines developed so some people were better off, but there was still a huge divide between rich and poor. In the 1950s and 1960s things got better. Prime Minister Harold Macmillan famously stated, 'You've never had it so good!' and for many that was true. By 1964, 90 per cent of British homes owned a television and Margaret Thatcher began a revolution in home ownership with her 'right to buy' policy in the 1980s.

Not everyone was included in this prosperity. There is still an underclass – some estimates suggest just as many as in 1900 – of those reliant on the state for help and benefits; unskilled or earning the minimum wage; poorly educated and thus the first to be made unemployed when economic 'boom' turns to 'bust'. The divide between rich and poor sometimes seems wider today than ever before. Food banks have spread around the country to try to help those unable to feed themselves. Many people feel alienated from society, living in poor housing and with few prospects to better themselves. Community spirit has often been lost and many, especially the elderly, feel alone and isolated. The debate over 'self-help' or 'government intervention' seems as apt today as in Victorian times.

SOURCE 1

From the British Parliamentary Papers, Shipping Casualties, ('Loss of the *Titanic*'), 1912

		Saved
Women	First class	97%
	Third Class	46%
Men	First Class	32%
	Third Class	16%

	Total saved
First class	62%
Second Class	61%
Third Class	25%
Crew	23%

FACTFILE

Means test

In an attempt to deal with unemployment the Government introduced the means test in 1931. The income of the whole family was taken into account to determine if benefits could be received. That meant that if a wife or daughter was working, the family's benefits were cut. Unemployed people hated it.

THINK

1 What do the figures in Source 1 tell us about Britain at the start of the twentieth century?
2 In your opinion, has everyone benefited equally from the vast increase in wealth since 1900?
3 Can everyone get free medical care 'from the cradle to the grave' today?
4 Study Source 2.
   a) What point is it making about life in Britain in 2014?
   b) Who does it say is poor in Britain today?
   c) How useful is this source in understanding wealth and poverty in Britain today?

SOURCE 2

A poster issued by Church Action on Poverty in 2014. It echoes a famous 1979 election poster by the Conservative Party with the slogan 'Labour isn't working'

4.2 Modern treatment of disease

FOCUS

At the start of the twentieth century child mortality remained high, and soldiers' deaths from infectious diseases in the Boer War were twice that of deaths from injuries or wounds.

But by the end of the century, medicine and the medical profession had made huge strides. New drugs were discovered, such as insulin and penicillin; better screening and diagnosis was introduced; medical research had become a major industry. This topic will look at the causes of these strides in medicine, how the profession dealt with new diseases, and how people responded to the changes.

Alexander Fleming: Did he discover penicillin?

Penicillin had been discovered in the nineteenth century. Indeed, Lister had used it once to treat infection in a wound, but had not published his notes.

During the First World War, Alexander Fleming observed that antiseptics seemed unable to prevent infection, especially in deep wounds. He decided to try to find something that would kill the microbes that caused infection. One of the most dangerous was staphylococci, which caused septicaemia. In 1928, on returning from holiday, he noticed a mould – penicillin – that had grown on one of his petri dishes. He also noticed that the staphylococci bacteria around the mould had been killed off. That was the start of the story of penicillin. Fleming called it an antibiotic, meaning 'destructive of life'. He published his results in 1929, but couldn't raise enough funds to develop the drug.

In 1937 Howard Florey and Ernst Chain, working at Oxford University, began to research penicillin after reading an article by Fleming. They overcame the difficulties of producing enough of the drug. They experimented first on mice, in 1940, and then on humans, in 1941. Their first trial, a policeman badly infected after being scratched by a rose bush, died after five days when their stock of the drug ran out, but the trial proved how effective penicillin was.

The Second World War provided a huge incentive to the development of the drug, and in 1943 it was used for the first time on Allied troops in North Africa, with great success. America and Britain jointly produced huge quantities of penicillin and without doubt it saved many lives in 1944 and 1945. After the war it was widely used to treat many illnesses like bronchitis, impetigo, pneumonia, tonsillitis, syphilis, meningitis, boils, abscesses and many other kinds of wounds. Fleming, Chain and Florey received the Nobel Prize for Medicine in 1945.

Other antibiotics followed, such as streptomycin in 1944, tetracycline in 1953 and mitomycin in 1956. Cortisone was developed in 1950 to treat arthritis. New vaccines emerged to treat polio and measles. TRANQUILISERS came on the market, and the birth control pill, too. There were new pills to treat depression, psychosis, hypertension, you name it; it seemed that medical research and scientific medicine had the answer to every health problem.

Alexander Fleming, 1881–1955

- Trained as a doctor and served in the Army Medical Corps during the First World War.
- He became professor of his medical school in 1928 and published many papers on bacteriology, immunology and chemotherapy.
- He was knighted for his work in 1944.
- He was jointly awarded the Nobel Prize in 1945 for his work on penicillin.

THINK

1 What part did chance play in the discovery of penicillin?
2 What part did war play in the development of penicillin?
3 Who, in your opinion, deserves the title 'father of penicillin'? Explain your answer.

SOURCE 1

A 1944 advert for penicillin

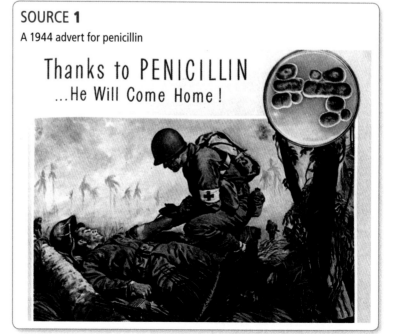

The 'Age of Pills'?

As new antibiotics and other medicines were produced, doctors were bombarded with literature about new drugs and free samples. There were fortunes to be made with a successful drug, and sometimes this led to companies taking shortcuts or inadequately testing the drugs before they were distributed. A perfect example of this is thalidomide, introduced in the 1950s as a mild sleeping pill, safe even for pregnant women to use. However, it led to thousands of babies worldwide being born with malformed limbs. It was 1962 before the link was made, and an acrimonious lawsuit before the German manufacturer and its British LICENSEE admitted blame and agreed to COMPENSATE victims. One positive outcome of the thalidomide controversy was the setting up of a much tougher testing and approval process for new drugs.

The role of the General Practitioner

Especially since 1948 when the Labour Government set up the National Health Service (page 89) the family doctor, or GP, has been central to the delivery of medical services. Source 2, by an American writer, sums up what people expected from their GP. Source 3 shows an alternative view of the role of the GP.

THINK

Study Source 2.

1 What medical services does this GP supply? Who carries out those services today?
2 What other advice does the GP give? Who carries out those services today?
3 Is this, in your opinion, a realistic or an idealised picture of the work of a family doctor?
4 This is an American source. Does that mean it is irrelevant to a study of the role of the GP in Britain in the 1950s and 1960s?

SOURCE 2

Carl Binger, writing in 1956, quoted in *The Greatest Benefit to Mankind* by Roy Porter (Fontana Press, 1999), p.669

[T]he family doctor delivered babies and supervised their nursing, their weaning and their teething, then he vaccinated them and saw them through their measles and chicken pox and whooping cough. He told the boy about the facts of life and treated the girl for her menstrual cramps. He advised about diet and rest, gave spring tonics, clipped tonsils, set a broken arm, reassured father who couldn't sleep because of business worries, pulled mother through a case of typhoid or double pneumonia, reprimanded cook who was found, on her day out, to have a dozen empty whiskey bottles in her clothes closet, gave advice about a young man's choice of college and profession, comforted grandma, who was losing her memory and becoming more and more irritable, and closed grandpa's eyes in his final sleep.

SOURCE 3

A twenty-first-century view of GPs by the cartoonist Richard Jolley

"Oh, that... that's the GP's motto."

A growing belief in alternative medicine

Controversies like the thalidomide case made some people distrust ORTHODOX MEDICINE, and there has been a huge increase in interest in what has become known as alternative or HOLISTIC MEDICINE. Treatments like hydrotherapy, aromatherapy, hypnotherapy and acupuncture became popular in some quarters. Many of them were based on old, traditional treatments using herbs and 'pure' treatments designed to work in harmony with the body, rather than using chemicals as a barrage against illness. Nearly every high street now includes its own health food shop where a wide range of alternative herbal remedies are sold.

Acupuncture, for example, is a traditional Chinese method of treating illness by sticking needles into various parts of the body and tapping into the natural flows of energy around the body. Prince Charles has long been a supporter of homeopathy, claiming, in a speech to the World Health Organization in Geneva in 2006, that it is 'rooted in ancient traditions that intuitively understood the need to maintain balance and harmony with our minds, bodies and the natural world'.

Not everyone agrees. The British Medical Association has described homeopathy as 'witchcraft' and Sir Mark Walport, Chief Scientific Advisor to the Government, speaking in 2013, dismissed it as 'nonsense'. The evidence appears conflicting, but nevertheless alternative medicine has a strong hold on many people who dislike the idea of filling one's body with chemicals.

What if you couldn't afford to see the doctor?

We have seen throughout this book that many people either chose *not* to visit a medical professional, or *could not* afford to. They relied on family remedies, or the local 'wise woman' to treat them. This hadn't changed for the first half of the twentieth century at least, as Source 5 shows.

SOURCE 5

From an interview with Kathleen Davys, describing growing up in Birmingham in the 1930s

Headaches, we had vinegar and brown paper, for whooping cough we had camphorated oil rubbed on our chests, or goose fat. For mumps we had stockings round our throats and for measles we had tea stewed in the teapot by the fire – all different kinds of home cures. They thought they were better than going to the doctor's. Well, they couldn't afford the doctor because sixpence in those days was like looking at a £5 note today.

Superbugs

Drug-resistant infections could lead to 10 million extra deaths a year worldwide – report

(The *Guardian*, 11 December 2014)

Perhaps the age of pills is coming to an end in the twenty-first century. More and more bacteria are becoming resistant to antibiotics as, according to some authorities, doctors continue to over-subscribe them for minor illnesses. Patients brought in to hospital for routine operations pick up infections that until recent times seemed trivial. Now, in the form of superbugs such as MRSA and the norovirus, they can be killers. Even the most modern, and powerful, antibiotics can no longer fight them. Will surgery be possible without antibiotics? Your work in Chapter 2 suggests it might not. Recently there was even a call for redesigning hospital wards, to make them more 'Victorian' and 'clean' in an effort to fight these so-called superbugs.

SOURCE 4

How one organisation promotes the idea of holistic medicine in the twenty-first century

Holistic Medicine – Healing the Total Person

Body – Exercise, yoga, physician, medication, diet, herbs, acupuncture
Mind – Psychotherapy, medication, rest, meditation, vacation
Spirit – Religion, pastor, master, yoga, meditation, acupuncture, vacation

THINK

5 What are the similarities between Source 4 and the Ancient Greek theory of the Four Humours?
6 You might remember the nursery rhyme 'Jack and Jill'. Jack went to bed to mend his head with vinegar and brown paper. Does that mean nursery rhymes are an accurate source of knowledge about medicine?
7 Discuss home cures with your grandparents. What did they use to cure common diseases?
8 Why do some people distrust modern medicine?
9 Why might the BMA call alternative medicine 'witchcraft'?
10 Why is there such a debate over 'alternative' medicine?
11 Why are antibiotics becoming less effective?

A case study: A visit by 'The Spanish Lady' in 1918–19

In 1918 a PANDEMIC spread around a war-weary world. An estimated 20–40 million people worldwide died as a result of the flu, which was a particularly devastating strain, evolved from bird flu and thought to originate in China. It is said to have infected 20 per cent of the world's population, and proved most deadly for 20–40-year-olds. Initially it was thought to be a result of German BIOLOGICAL WARFARE, or an effect of prolonged trench warfare and the use of mustard gas. What is clear is that mass troop movements in 1918 at the end of the war, helped rapidly transmit the disease across the globe. Homecoming troops then spread the disease to the civilian population.

In Britain the Government imposed censorship about the spread of the infection in a bid to prevent panic, but newspapers *were* allowed to report the 7 million deaths in Spain, hence the name given to the disease: Spanish Flu, or 'The Spanish Lady'. A visit from 'the Lady' could be deadly: apparently healthy people at breakfast time could be dead by tea time. In a post-war weary and weakened population it spread rapidly, but no one knew why. Symptoms were quite general at first: headaches, sore throat, loss of appetite. Those who recovered seemed to do so quickly, so the outbreak was originally known as 'Three-Day Fever'. Hospitals could not cope. There were no recognised treatments and no antibiotics. In a few months around 280,000 people died in the UK, mostly young men and women. Up to 20 per cent of those infected, died. Australian troops were stationed at Sutton Veny in Wiltshire from 1915 to 1919, and there was a military hospital there. Part of the cemetery is now a Commonwealth War Graves Commission site. Many Australian victims of the flu epidemic are buried there.

SOURCE 7
A children's skipping song, 1918–19

I had a little bird,
It's name was Enza.
I opened a window
and in-flu-enza

SOURCE 6
Headstones marking the graves of Canadian soldiers who fell victim to the flu epidemic, St Margarets, Clwyd

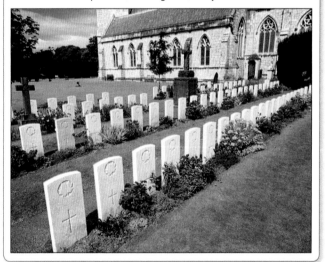

The General Medical Council suggested wearing a gauze mask over nose and mouth to prevent infection. Other suggested precautions included keeping children away from sick adults, gargling with salt water, boiling your handkerchiefs and staying in bed. Plenty of other options were on offer too: drink no alcohol or drink lots of alcohol; give up smoking; drink lots of beef tea – OXO spent a fortune advertising how it 'fortified the system and increased nutrition'. Most people resorted to their usual medicine cupboard remedies: laudanum, opium, quinine, rhubarb, treacle or vinegar. None, of course, could cure the flu but some things could help alleviate the symptoms.

THINK
1 Is it accurate to compare the 1918–19 flu epidemic with the Black Death (see page 26)?
2 How similar, and how different, are people's reactions to the two pandemics?
3 What can we learn about twentieth-century medicine from the flu epidemic?

TOPIC SUMMARY
Modern treatment of disease
- The discovery of antibiotics made a huge impact on disease in the twentieth century.
- Pharmaceutical companies developed new drugs throughout the century.
- Some drugs, like thalidomide, had harmful side effects.
- Some diseases are becoming resistant to antibiotics.
- Many people turned to alternative medicine to cure their illnesses.
- The first port of call if you were sick became the GP surgery.
- Some people now question whether scientific medicine has all the answers to conquering disease.

PROGRESS CHECK
Significance
1 How significant is the discovery of penicillin in the development of medicine in the twentieth century?

Now answer this question:
2 To what extent have antibiotics made health for all an achievable goal in the twentieth century?

4.3 The impact of war and technology on surgery

FOCUS

War is a great engine of change and the medical advances that took place during the two world wars, and after, were immense. Since 1945, and especially since the 1960s, technology has transformed surgery: transplants, keyhole surgery, replacement limbs, IVF, and even cloned animals, have completely changed both what surgeons can do and success rates. This topic explores these developments, but also considers the opinions held by some that technology has gone too far, and that ethics need to be re-established and boundaries reset.

In what ways did the First World War change surgery?

The First World War was the first major conflict where deaths from injuries outweighed deaths from disease. Over 8 million soldiers died, and more than 20 million were injured. In the face of such massive numbers medical services at the Front had to adapt.

From 1915 Casualty Clearing Stations (CCS) were set up as near to the Front as they could be. Emphasis was placed on evacuating casualties as quickly as possible. Injuries were split into three types: slightly wounded, who were quickly given necessary treatment and sent back to the Front; those needing hospital care; and those beyond help (see Source 1).

SOURCE 2

From *A Nurse at the Front – the First World War Diaries of Sister Edith Appleton* (Simon & Schuster, 2013)

July 4 [1916]

Wounded! Hundreds upon hundreds on stretchers, being carried, walking – all covered from head to foot in well-caked mud. The rush and buzz of ambulances and motor-buses is the only thing I can remember of yesterday outside my wards. Inside it took us longer than the whole day to anything like cope with the work of changing, feeding and dressing the wounds of our share of them. We had horribly bad wounds in numbers – some crawling with maggots, some stinking and tense with gangrene. One poor lad had both eyes shot through and they were all smashed and mixed up with eyelashes. He was quite calm, and very tired. He said, 'Shall I need an operation? I can't see anything'. Poor boy, he never will.

SOURCE 1

How injured soldiers were evacuated and treated during the First World War

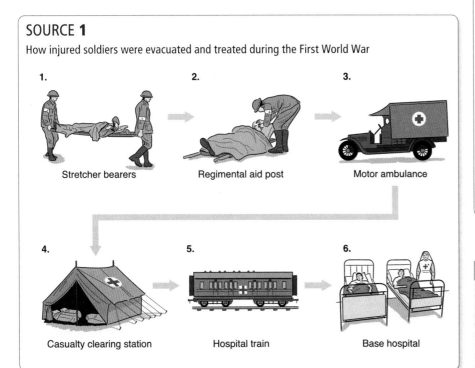

1. Stretcher bearers
2. Regimental aid post
3. Motor ambulance
4. Casualty clearing station
5. Hospital train
6. Base hospital

THINK

1   What, according to Source 2, were the major challenges facing the Royal Army Medical Corps during the First World War?
2   How well did they seem to be coping in July 1916?

Technological strides

New technology made a great difference. Mobile X-ray units allowed better identification of items inside the body of an injured soldier; blood transfusions were pioneered by the British Army, and by 1917 blood was being stockpiled and stored for up to 28 days, ready for instant use. New techniques such as the Thomas Splint were developed, used for dealing with a broken leg. In 1914, 80 per cent of soldiers with a broken femur died but by 1916, 80 per cent survived. Improvements were made in both cleaning deep wounds and in keeping them clean. Convalescent wards and hospitals were set up in England, all focused on getting injured soldiers fit enough to return to the Front.

Shell-shock treatment

Between 1914 and 1918, the British Army identified 80,000 men with what would now be defined as the symptoms of shell-shock. A total of 306 British and Commonwealth soldiers were executed by firing squad because, initially, the condition was classed as desertion or cowardice. These executions remained contentious, until 2006, when a law pardoned those who had been executed. Later in the war the condition known as shell-shock was accepted, and many, especially officers, were treated at hospitals like Craiglockhart, near Edinburgh. Here, William Rivers, a psychologist, developed the 'talking cure' which helped many come to terms with their experiences. The 'talking cure' was combined with lots of healthy sports and craft activities, as a kind of occupational therapy. Perhaps the most famous patients treated at Craiglockhart were the 'War Poets' Siegfried Sassoon and Wilfred Owen. This technique became more widely used after the war in treating mental illnesses.

Skin grafts

As a result of the fighting, many soldiers suffered facial injuries, and Harold Gillies developed ground-breaking new techniques for treating these. By 1917 he had persuaded the army to set up a special hospital for facial repairs. Over 5,000 servicemen were treated by Gillies and his colleagues, often requiring many operations to graft existing skin onto injuries. His techniques even enabled him to reconstruct damaged faces (see Source 3). He is regarded as the pioneer of plastic surgery, and was knighted after the war.

THINK

1 Which do you think was the biggest medical innovation of the First World War? Why?
2 Which do you think would be most useful after the war had ended?

SOURCE 3

Four photographs showing the facial reconstruction of a soldier wounded during the Battle of the Somme, 1916, reported by Harold Gillies, 1920

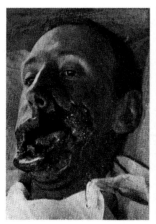

In what ways did technology change surgery?

X-ray technology

X-rays were discovered, by accident, in 1895 by Wilhelm Roentgen. They allowed doctors to see inside the patient and quickly became an essential diagnostic tool. Roentgen refused to patent the technology so their use rapidly spread around the known world, especially after further inventions by Edison that allowed images to be captured on glass plates and by George Eastman in 1918 who introduced X-ray film.

SOURCE 4

A double-focus X-ray tube, 1896

Between the wars scientists worked to develop radiotherapy as a tool for targeting cancerous cells inside the body, often thereby avoiding the need for invasive surgery. They also extended the range of X-ray imaging, using CT scans (computerised tomography) that allow surgeons to see tissue as well as bone in three-dimensional images. A recent survey of doctors voted CT scans as *the* most essential tool in a surgeon's armoury for fighting illness.

Blood transfusions

Although there had been many attempts to transfer blood from person to person, most were unsuccessful, until in 1901 Karl Landsteiner, an Austrian, discovered different blood groups. Once donor and recipient blood types could be matched transfusions became more practical. Initially, blood had to be delivered directly from the donor to the patient, making the process very difficult. But it was later discovered that if you added an anti-coagulant to the blood, and kept it cold, blood could be stored for up to 28 days before use. In October 1915 on the Western Front the first 'blood banks' were set up in anticipation of battle casualties.

In 1921 the British Red Cross set up the first voluntary blood donor scheme and this was copied throughout the world. In 1938, as preparation for the Second World War, the British Government set up the Army Blood Supply Depot in Bristol. This was kept supplied by as many as 700,000 blood donors during the war. The voluntary system of donating blood still applies today. In 1940 it was discovered how to make blood plasma, in effect dehydrated blood, making blood easier to store and transport. Later in the war, plastic wallets replaced glass bottles.

THINK

3   Is it war or technology that is most responsible for progress in X-rays and blood transfusions?
4   Which tool, in your opinion, is the more powerful in helping surgeons?

The Second World War and beyond

Perhaps the most famous surgeon of the Second World War was Sir Archibald McIndoe. His work on burns included treating pilots shot down during the Battle of Britain. He improved upon Gillies' techniques for skin grafting and his patients set up the 'Guinea Pig Club' to celebrate his work. McIndoe also spent a lot of time and effort helping his patients reintegrate into society despite their disfigurements.

There were continued improvements in blood transfusion, and Sir Harold Ridley, treating Allied airmen, found that perspex splinters were not always rejected by the eye and this led to the development of cataract surgery.

Much effort was also put into preventative measures: mepacrine was developed as an effective anti-malaria tablet; rations were carefully balanced to ensure a healthy diet; effective gas masks were issued as defence against chemical warfare; deep shelters were built as protection against bombing. During the Korean War (1950–53) Mobile Army Surgical Hospital (MASH) units were established by the USA, taking experienced surgeons as near the battlefield as possible, thus reducing the time between injury and treatment. This principle has been extended further in Iraq and Afghanistan by the British Army, and consequently many more injured troops survive.

ACTIVITY

1   Make a list of developments in medicine that have made it more likely that injured troops will survive.
2   Discuss your list with your neighbour. Can you agree which developments are most significant?

1 Look carefully at this photograph of modern surgery (Source 5). Compare it with Source 4 on page 20. Find all the items in the operating theatre in Source 5 that in your opinion make surgery safer.

2 Compare this image to that on page 36 (Topic 2.2) and Fanny Burney's account of her surgery (Topic 2.3, page 37) in 1811. Draw up a table like the one below and complete it to show what has changed and what has stayed the same in surgery over the last 300 years.

Stayed the same	Changed

3 Now consider the similarities and differences in surgery over the last 300 years.
   a) Which is the greatest similarity?
   b) Which, in your opinion, is the greatest change?
   c) Can you explain why these changes have occurred?

Technology in control

SOURCE 5

Inside a modern operating theatre

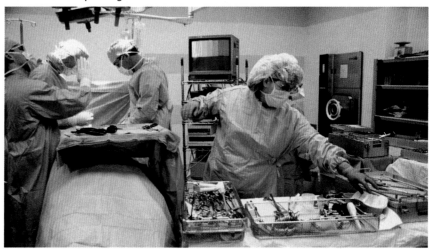

The activity (left) will have shown you that there have been huge changes in the way surgery is carried out, and in its success rates. There have also been major changes in the *types* of surgery undertaken. Throughout much of the twentieth century, radiation therapy has been used to treat cancerous cells, making them easier to target as technology has refined the technique. In 1952 the first kidney transplant took place. In 1961 the first heart pacemaker, a mechanical device that keeps the heart pumping blood around the body, was developed. In 1967 the first heart transplant operation took place in Cape Town, South Africa, by Dr Christian Barnard. His patient lived for eighteen days. Now, they are routine: in 2014, 181 heart transplant operations took place in England alone. Hip replacements were introduced in 1972 bringing mobility to many who previously had found walking difficult. Louise Brown became the world's first test-tube baby in 1978, an operation bringing hope to many childless couples desperate for a baby.

Imaging technology plays a huge part in earlier, clearer diagnosis of illness, thereby increasing the chances of recovery. Non-invasive surgery – using radiation or minimally-invasive surgery using a miniature camera inserted into the mouth or other orifices, allowing a surgeon to see inside their patient without cutting open the body – are now the everyday reality of surgery.

Keyhole surgery, through a very small cut in the body, is now commonplace, reducing the intrusiveness of operating on someone. Laser treatment, especially for eye operations and many cancers, is now widespread, taking only a fraction of the time operations previously took and with less invasive damage and quicker healing time. There are even robotic operation systems licensed in the USA. Mortality rates from operations are carefully monitored, and there are even 'league tables' for hospitals and surgeons so patients can choose the 'best' place for their treatment.

Better understanding, increased demand

Technology has also aided disease diagnosis. CAT scans, MRI scans and endoscopes (tubes inserted into the body which contain miniature cameras) all allow surgeons to 'see' inside a person without the need to cut them open. The discovery of DNA in 1953 and the subsequent 'human genome' project have all enhanced the medical profession's understanding of how the body works and how to make it better when it is malfunctioning.

1 What part has technology played in changing surgery in the last 50 years?

2 Has this made it easier to keep everyone healthy, or harder? Explain your answer.

The establishment of the National Health Service in 1948 by the Labour Government (see page 89) created a demand and a feeling of entitlement to medical services never felt before. This continues to increase, making it difficult for hospitals to deliver. New technology and new drugs are expensive, meaning some are not approved for use by the NHS, leading to claims that services are being rationed. Waiting lists exist for most operations, although recent governments have made a great effort to reduce these.

Too much interference?

Such are the advances in medicine that some people today argue that science and technology have gone too far. They suggest it is one thing to operate on someone when they are ill, but it is not right to help childless couples have a baby, or perhaps choose the sex of their baby. There have been reports of abortions of girl foetuses, because the couple involved only wanted a boy, and of an illegal trade in kidneys and other organs 'stolen' from poor people in other parts of the world. If you have studied the Nazis you will know that they carried out experiments on concentration camp inmates, and introduced compulsory STERILISATION for people they deemed as 'inferior', who did not fit their 'Master Race' ideology. Experiments in CLONING have taken place: 'Dolly the Sheep' was the world's first successfully cloned animal in 1996 in Scotland. It was part of an experiment to develop human medicines in the milk of farm animals. The next step, although not currently legal, could be using the same technique to clone humans, perhaps to prevent the transmission of disease from mother to child. Where is the boundary between treating disease and creating life?

> ### SOURCE 6
> From *Discover Magazine*, February 2015
>
> #### UK Becomes First Country to Approve 'Three-Parent Babies'
>
> *On Tuesday, the UK's House of Commons voted 382 to 128 in favour of the controversial technique, called mitochondrial donation, and the first 'three-person baby' could be conceived later this year. Doctors say mitochondrial donation will prevent mothers from transferring incurable genetic diseases to their children. Opponents have raised ethical concerns, saying it sets humanity on the slippery slope toward 'designer babies'. Church groups in the UK lobbied for parliament to oppose the new law. They oppose the destruction of human EMBRYOS, and worry that the law opens a Pandora's box of genetic tinkering.*

SOURCE 7
A cartoon examining the new technique of mitochondrial donation, 2012

She's got my eyes, her father's nose and the donor's chance of not contracting my disease...

Whatever we might think about these current medical controversies it is clear that in the last 100 years or so surgery has changed out of all recognition. It has become much safer, less painful and much better at 'fixing' human medical problems.

> **THINK**
>
> Study Sources 6 and 7.
>
> 3 What are the arguments in favour of three-parent babies?
> 4 What are the arguments against three-parent babies?
> 5 What does the issue tell us about the role of surgery today?

> **TOPIC SUMMARY**
>
> ### The impact of war and technology on surgery
> - War, particularly the First World War, brought huge changes to the way injured soldiers were treated.
> - These changes spilled over into peacetime.
> - Technology has continued to change surgery, increasingly so over the last 50 years.
> - The mortality rate for surgery has fallen dramatically during the last 100 years.
> - The expense of many kinds of surgery is now a real issue for society.
> - Just because some types of surgery are *possible* doesn't mean they are *desirable*. Modern surgery raises many issues for debate in society.

> **PROGRESS CHECK**
>
> ### Causes and factors
> 1 In your opinion, has technology or war been the biggest factor for change in the twentieth century?
>
> ### Significance
> 2 Whose work was the most significant in the development of surgery, William Rivers or Harold Gillies?

4.4 Modern public health

FOCUS

The twentieth century has seen a major shift in the role of government with regards to public health. The Victorian *laissez-faire* attitude has been replaced by an acceptance that it is the role of government to ensure people live healthy lives. However, the extent of that role is still open to debate, even today. Changes in poverty and housing in post-war society eventually led to the creation of the NHS, taking care of people 'from cradle to grave'. This topic examines the costs involved in modern-day healthcare, the differences in treatment that still exist because of those costs, and our responsibilities as users of a healthcare system for all.

Identifying the problem

We have already seen on page 53 how so many Boer War recruits were unfit to serve in the army. This was a shock to many people at the time, and led to worries about the continued growth of the economy and strength of the Empire. The state of these volunteers for the army provided the inspiration to investigate living conditions and the health of ordinary people in the new industrial cities, which eventually led to the changes introduced by the Liberal Government from 1906 (see page 87). As a result, some social surveys were carried out in order to understand the extent of the problem. Charles Booth, in his *Life and Labour of the People* published in 1889, found that 35 per cent of London's population was living in abject poverty. His detailed survey had originally been designed to prove the belief that 25 per cent of the population lived in poverty was far too high!

PROFILES

Charles Booth, 1840–1916

- Booth discovered the level of poverty in parts of Liverpool when campaigning unsuccessfully for election to Parliament in 1865.
- Best known for his investigations into and documenting of poverty in London in the 1880s and 1890s.
- His published reports were very influential in changing attitudes towards the poor.

Seebohm Rowntree, 1871–1954

- A Quaker, he was born into the rich family of chocolate makers in York.
- Rowntree was inspired by the work of Booth to investigate poverty in York.
- He was a successful businessman all his life, overseeing the expansion of the family firm.
- He became very influential in government circles, influencing not just Lloyd George but Beveridge and his report in 1942.
- He could perhaps be said to have single-handedly changed government attitudes to poverty forever.

Seebohm Rowntree was inspired by Booth's work to do the same in York, where he lived. In 1897 and 1898 his researchers interviewed over 46,000 citizens of the city, and his results were published in *Poverty, A Study in Town Life*, in 1901. He found that very nearly half of the working-class people in York lived in poverty. He is acknowledged as the inventor of the term 'poverty line', and became an adviser to Lloyd George after 1906.

A third book played an influential part in shifting opinion. In 1913 Maud Pember Reeves published *Round About a Pound A Week*, a detailed study of the way workers, many of them in regular employment, like policemen, struggled to exist on an average wage of £1 a week. She had set out to prove that these families wasted money on drink but found that often women were going without food so the man (the wage earner) and the children could eat.

What were the achievements of the Liberal Government of 1906–14?

Here is a list of just some of the legislation passed by the Liberal Government.

Year	Act passed	Effect of legislation
1906	Workmen's Compensation Act	Granted compensation for injury at work
	Education (Provision of Meals) Act	Introduced free school meals
1907	Education (Administrative Provisions) Act	Created school medical inspections
	Matrimonial Causes Act	Maintenance payments to be paid to divorced women
1908	Children and Young Person's Act (Children's Charter)	Made it illegal to sell alcohol, tobacco or fireworks to children
	Old-Age Pensions Act	Over 70s received 5 shillings a week, 7s 6d for a married couple
1909	Labour Exchanges Act	Helped get people back into a job
	Housing and Town Planning Act	Made it illegal to build back-to-back houses
1911	National Insurance Act	Sick and unemployment pay introduced if you paid contributions into the scheme

In introducing the 1909 Budget, Lloyd George stated:

> This is a war budget … to wage implacable warfare against poverty and squalidness.

But did these measures have as much impact as he stated they would? Medical inspections were introduced in 1907, but poor families could not afford to pay for necessary treatment. Pensions were introduced for over 70s (the average age of death was around 50), but only if you had worked all your life and could prove you were not a drunkard. The National Insurance scheme only applied if you paid regular contributions, but part of the cause of poverty was irregular employment. And so on.

The 1909 Budget was thrown out in the House of Lords by the Conservative peers, who were opposed to paying for these reforms. It caused a constitutional crisis. Even some Liberals thought they were too expensive. And others, like the newly formed Labour Party, felt they didn't go far enough.

FACTFILE

Poverty line

The minimum level of income that is thought necessary for someone or a family to live on at the time. Today, in Britain, this is set at those earning less than 60 per cent of the average wage.

THINK

1 Why were the three books mentioned here so influential at the time?
2 How similar, and how different, are the problems identified by these three authors to those identified by Edwin Chadwick and Thomas Southwood Smith in Topic 3.4 (page 68)?

FACTFILE

The value of money in 1908

5 shillings = 25p

7s 6d = 37.5p

Remember, Maud Pember Reeves' book suggested workers struggled on wages of £1 per week at this time.

THINK

3 Why were the Liberal reforms so divisive?
4 Which of the reforms do you think might be most successful? Why?

A case study: School meals in Bradford

SOURCE 1

Serving free school meals at a school in Bradford, October 1907

THINK

Study Source 2.

1 What happens to children's weight in term time?
2 What happens to children's weight in holiday time?
3 Does this source suggest providing free school meals for 'necessitous children' worked?
4 Does this source prove that the Liberal welfare reforms worked?

Dr Barnardo had provided very cheap or free meals for the children attending his 'Ragged School' in London (see page 68), arguing that children could not learn properly if they were malnourished. Manchester and Bradford local authorities had introduced school meals for 'necessitous children' and led the campaign for the introduction of school meals nationally. One of the first things the Liberal Government did in 1906 was to introduce free school meals, but it was not compulsory for local authorities to provide them until 1914, when 14 million were served over the course of the year. Parents could be asked to make a contribution towards the cost if they could afford it, and the rest of the money had to come from local rates.

During the Second World War around 15 per cent of the school population was receiving free school meals, others had to pay around 5d or 6d for a meal. Gradually, the price increased. In 1988 the right to free school meals was restricted by Margaret Thatcher's government. In September 2014 the Coalition Government of David Cameron and Nick Clegg re-introduced free school meals for Key Stage 1 children, partly as a result of concerns that many children were not learning properly because they were so hungry. This is not dissimilar to the reasons why Dr Barnardo established his Ragged School.

SOURCE 2

Extract from a report by the City of Bradford Medical Officer on the effects of school meals, 1907

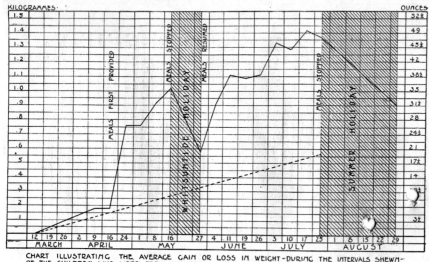

CHART ILLUSTRATING THE AVERAGE GAIN OR LOSS IN WEIGHT DURING THE INTERVALS SHEWN OF THE CHILDREN WHO WERE FED. THE BROKEN LINE SHEWS THE AVERAGE INCREASE IN WEIGHT DURING THE SAME TIME OF THE CONTROL CHILDREN.

The War and after

We have already seen some of the impact of the First World War on health (pages 81–82). One historian, Corelli Barnett, wrote in 2003:

> For the majority of soldiers actual living conditions in and behind the lines on quiet sectors were little if any worse than in peacetime. Certainly many British soldiers enjoyed a better diet, better medical care and better welfare than they had as civilians.

(From *The Great War* by Corelli Barnett, BBC Books, 2003)

It may seem hard to believe that war conditions for a soldier could actually be better than during peacetime, but Barnett's words illustrate just how bad living conditions were for some people, despite the Liberal Government's reforms.

During the Second World War, the population was also organised by the Government but this time provision was made for a better life for people after the war. In 1942 William Beveridge, an economist who had been an advisor to Lloyd George from 1906 to 1914, published the Beveridge Report. This set out proposals for change after the war was won, to fight the five 'Giant Evils' of 'Want, Disease, Ignorance, Squalor and Idleness'. Clement Attlee, the new Labour prime minister in 1945, agreed to implement these ideas and create a true Welfare State. Part of this was the introduction of the National Health Service in 1948. For the first time, hospitals, doctors, nurses, pharmacists, opticians and dentists were brought together under one umbrella organisation to provide services that were free for all at the point of delivery. The aim was to provide support 'from the cradle to the grave' financed out of taxation. Another part of the Welfare State was a comprehensive system of benefits, building on those introduced in 1911, but still based on contributions made by workers.

It will be no surprise to discover that many medical professionals were totally opposed to the introduction of the NHS, seeing it as an attempt to curtail their livelihood and their rights to treat whoever they liked. Churchill, leader of the Conservative Party, said it was 'a curse on the country' and that it discouraged voluntary efforts. One poll carried out by the British Medical Association found only 10 per cent of doctors in favour of the NHS. Nye Bevan, as Minister of Health, had the job of overseeing the birth of the NHS, introducing decent healthcare for all and transforming millions of lives. Despite all the difficulties, on 4 July 1948 the NHS was born.

Demand for healthcare was huge, much greater than expected, showing how poor the health of most ordinary people was. In 1950 the budget was under pressure and in 1952 charges for spectacles were introduced, prescriptions cost 1 shilling, and dental treatment £1. It was the end of a completely free NHS.

SOURCE 3

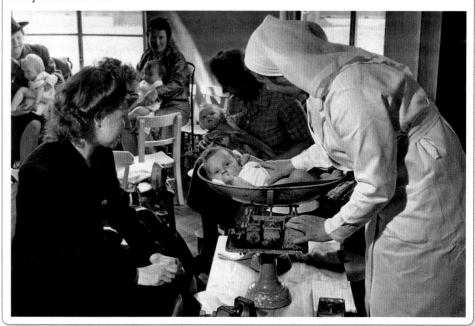

A baby being weighed in a Bristol clinic, 1948. This was one of the free services provided by the newly established NHS

THINK

5 How might men in the army during the First World War be healthier than at home, as Corelli Barnett argues?

6 What does the impact of the introduction of the NHS tell us about the health of most people in the 1920s and 1930s?

7 Why was a completely free NHS unsustainable?

Medical moments in time: London, 1935

ACTIVITY

1 Look carefully at the picture. Can you identify:
   a) the impact of any changes introduced by the Liberal Government
   b) examples of medical progress?
2 Compare this picture of London in 1935 with the picture of London in 1848 (pages 64–65). Copy and complete the following table to show evidence of continuity and of change in medicine over this period.

Evidence of continuity in medicine, 1848–1935	Evidence of change in medicine, 1848–1935

3 Write a paragraph to summarise the progress in health in twentieth-century London.

I wish I didn't have to charge for visits and medicines. Many people can't afford to pay so never see a doctor.
FINE PIES
Now then, mothers. This class helps you keep your children healthy. Remember the law says that you must get your children vaccinated. Let's start with keeping your babies clean.
But we haven't finished paying him for the last time.
Jill's got measles. I'd better call the doctor.
We have to. The girl down the road got measles and now she's deaf in one ear.
Don't play out in the cold in bare feet. No wonder they hurt.
SCHOOL
Mother used hot turnip mash to treat chilblains. No need for anything else.

Clean air, new towns and tower blocks: The definitive answer to public health?

In December 1952, London was engulfed in what became known as the 'killer smog'. Air pollution and fumes from coal fires were trapped by an ANTICYCLONE over the city from 5–9 December. Recent estimates suggest over 12,000 people died and as many as 100,000 were taken ill as a result. It was the worst example of air pollution in Britain and led to the Government passing Clean Air Acts in 1956 and 1968. This encouraged householders throughout the country to change from coal fires to the cleaner gas and electricity, or even burn coke and other smokeless fuels.

New towns and cities were also developed, like Milton Keynes and Telford. This was an attempt to move people out of dirty, overcrowded neighbourhoods into 'greener' settings, with industry and housing carefully segregated. The first new town, at Letchworth, was the work of Ebenezer Howard, in 1903. Housing was meant to be attractive and spacious, gardens were an integral part of the plan, as were public parks and amenities. Cycle routes and pedestrian walkways were separated from traffic, to make travel safer for all. By 2014 over 2.7 million people lived in new towns or cities in the UK.

In the 1960s, slum clearance took place in old towns and cities, too, with a massive expansion of council-built housing in an attempt to provide everyone with a decent home. Unfit housing was demolished and often replaced with 'modern' tower blocks: high-rise blocks of flats with all modern conveniences like central heating, bathrooms and fitted kitchens.

Towns like Chelmsley Wood, just outside Birmingham, sprung up. Created in 1965 on a GREENFIELD SITE, it had over 16,000 homes designed to house 50,000 people who were unable to get a home in the city. At the time it was the largest single residential development in Europe.

ACTIVITY

1 Carry out your own research on a new town that has been proposed or is being built near where you live.
2 How is it similar, and how is it different, to the new towns of the 1960s?

THINK

1 What image of Cumbernauld is Source 4 designed to show? Does this provide useful evidence about public health in the 1960s?
2 How successful have the planners been at building better communities for people to live in during the twentieth century?

SOURCE 4

A view of new town housing in Cumbernauld, 1970, built to solve the severe shortage of housing in post-war Glasgow

Healthcare in the twenty-first century

Study Source 5; you have already come across the information in Source 4, on page 8, where you were asked if you thought these were young people's diseases or old people's. The truth is that cancer and heart disease, the major killers, can strike anyone at any age, whereas dementia is largely an older person's disease.

We have never been so well-fed, well-housed and well-off, so why are these diseases still so prevalent?

Unhealthy lifestyles?

> Just one can of fizzy drink a day can increase the risk of heart attack by a third and dramatically raise the chance of diabetes and stroke, the largest ever study has found. The study ... follows new official UK advice which says adults should restrict their sugar intake to just 30 grams – seven teaspoons – a day.

(*Daily Telegraph*, 28 September 2015)

It seems stories like these appear in the news nearly every day. Scientists estimate that many of us are reducing our life expectancy by our lifestyle. We eat too much, often of the wrong foods, drink too much alcohol, don't take enough exercise, and smoke too much. We also spend too much time sitting at a desk or playing computer games rather than exercising. All this adds up to a recipe for obesity and ill-health. Obesity is one of the greatest causes of heart disease. So despite better diagnoses of illness, the availability of more effective medicines and skilled surgeons, it is all to no avail if we refuse to follow a healthy lifestyle.

Prevention or cure?

Throughout the twentieth century, governments have put more and more effort into health education, trying to persuade people to live healthier lifestyles and look after themselves better. Some people argue it is not the job of government to do this; remember the letter to the *Times* newspaper at the time of the cholera outbreak (page 68)? Some people still think like that, arguing it is up to each individual to make their own choices. Others argue that there is a cost associated with poor lifestyle choices. For example, if people stopped smoking this would save the NHS millions of pounds each year. As fewer people would get sick, they would miss less time off work, and so this would help the economy grow. This argument applies to almost every aspect of health. Some people argue it is better to spend money on prevention than on curing diseases that could be prevented. These are the same arguments that the Victorians were having (see page 68) when Chadwick and Southwood Smith were saying much the same thing.

SOURCE 5

Killer diseases of late twentieth-century Britain (Source: Office of National Statistics)

Cancer
Heart disease
Respiratory disease (e.g. flu)
Liver disease
Dementia/Alzheimer's disease
Accidents

THINK

3 Study Source 5. To what extent are the killer diseases of the twentieth century similar to, and different from, the killer diseases of earlier times?

4 How easy is it to live a healthy lifestyle?

5 What's your view? Should money be spent on the prevention of disease rather than curing it? Isn't this a big change in the approach to healthcare?

SOURCE 6

One modern view of a healthy lifestyle

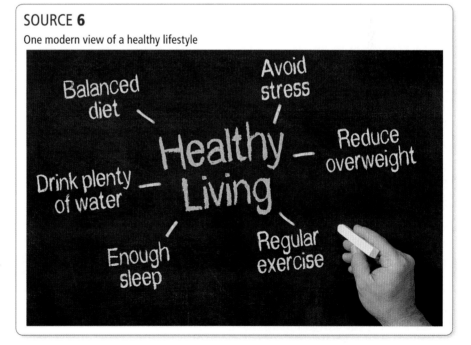

SOURCE 7

The cost, in health terms, of obesity and inactivity

150,000 people have a stroke each year.

In 2009, one in three deaths were due to cardiovascular disease.

2.34 million people in the UK have Type 2 diabetes.

Current levels of obesity could lead to 17,000 cases of cancer each year.

Every year this costs us £15.8 billion, which could buy 211 hospitals, 790 schools or 632,000 nurses.

THINK

1 Do you think it should it be the job of government to provide healthcare?
2 How should such healthcare be paid for?
3 If there is not enough money to treat everybody, who should get priority?

PROGRESS CHECK

Causes and factors

1 What role did wars play in changing the government's role in healthcare?

Similarities and differences

2 Compare Source 4 (page 92) with Doré's engraving of London in 1872 (Source 2, page 66). What are the similarities and differences between life in these two places?

Now answer this question:

3 How effectively, in your opinion, has Britain addressed the issue of public health in the twentieth century?

The development of new drugs in Britain

The Medical Research Council has set up an 'Innovation Fund' to help scientists develop new products. Currently scientists in universities who have received these funds are working on, among other things:

● the development of a new dressing for burns that detects infection and allows early treatment
● a new type of flu vaccine that would be effective against all types of flu
● a 'home test kit' to help patients decide if they have lung disease, which should help reduce the need for antibiotics.

Other new drugs and products are developed commercially by drug companies who, of course, are profit-led. An effective drug to treat AIDS, for example, which sold at a reasonable price, could make a fortune. So it is important that new products are very carefully tested and approved before use. As that process is expensive, it is often only major drug companies who can afford to produce these drugs.

Government policy can inadvertently lead to a shortage of some drugs. By refusing to pay high prices, or insisting that only cheaper versions of a drug are approved, the NHS can save millions of pounds. But it doesn't always work. In a recent case in Britain the drug company Roche stopped production of the drug clonazepam, used in RESPITE CARE for those in pain, claiming it could not make any money from the price the NHS was prepared to pay. The product now has to be imported and the price has risen from 67p an injection to £33. So in some health authorities use of the drug is now rationed.

As medicine is often very expensive, the healthcare trusts that run hospitals, and GPs, have to decide upon priorities. Some drugs and treatments are available in some areas, but not in others, leading to what newspapers are calling a 'postcode lottery' for treatment. Sometimes it seems the deciding factor in your treatment is not how ill you are but where you live.

Can we still afford an NHS?

The premise behind this course throughout has been that medical care and health have been getting better since AD1000. New discoveries, new methods, new drugs and treatments, even new attitudes, have supposedly transformed the lives and health of everyone in Britain. Yet arguments still rage about the cost of healthcare; of the role of the individual in providing healthcare for themselves; and the place of the state in providing healthcare. Especially in a time of AUSTERITY, when government spending has been cut back in most areas, there have been demands for the NHS to 'live within its means'. Some diseases, long thought of as conquered, like measles and rickets, are beginning to re-appear in our towns and cities.

TOPIC SUMMARY

Modern public health

● Careful investigation work showed how bad many people's living conditions were.
● The Liberal Government of 1906–14 introduced some changes, although the impact was smaller than hoped.
● War increased government intervention in people's lives.
● The Labour Government of 1945 introduced the NHS and completely transformed healthcare and the provision of services.
● Not all changes since 1945 have been for the better: tower blocks were often disliked.
● Nevertheless there have been great improvements in public health throughout the twentieth century.

4.5 Pulling it all together:
Modern-day Britain

A case study of the fight against AIDS

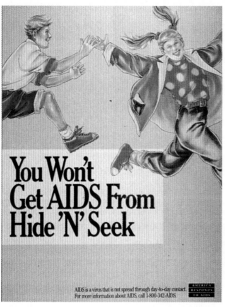

AIDS, or Acquired Immune Deficiency Syndrome, was first identified in 1981 in the USA when doctors noticed that large numbers of homosexuals were dying from causes that couldn't easily be identified. It took until 1983 for scientists to discover that a viral infection was attacking the immune system that protects the body from disease. Since then AIDS has become, according to some authorities, a pandemic, spreading across the world like the Black Death or cholera. By 2014 it was estimated that 40 million people around the world had died from AIDS, and that another 40 million are living with the disease.

In the UK there are over 100,000 people, mostly young, living with AIDS, and it is believed 25 per cent of them have no idea that they have the disease.

It is thought that AIDS originated among primates in Central Africa, and spread to humans there around the turn of the twentieth century. People do not die of AIDS, but often from catching very simple infections, like common colds, because the weakened immune system cannot fight off infection. AIDS is usually caused by having unprotected sex, with a male or a female who has the disease; by sharing hypodermic needles; by contaminated blood transfusions; and from mother to child during pregnancy or breast-feeding. Freddie Mercury, lead singer of *Queen*, is just one of many high-profile people who have died from having the disease.

So far there is no cure for AIDS. The best prevention is always practising safe sex, and not sharing needles, spoons or other drug-taking equipment. Drug companies worldwide are spending millions of pounds trying to develop a cure, so far without success. But most people, with their strong belief in scientific medicine, believe it is only a matter of time before a cure is discovered. The best that has been achieved so far is the ability to slow down the impact of the disease on the body, by using anti-viral therapy and drugs. These are extremely expensive, so in many countries treatment is unavailable to many. Without treatment people live on average nine to eleven years with the disease.

As you can tell, AIDS is very much a disease of a modern lifestyle. Sex and drugs play a large part, but not the only part, in spreading AIDS both within the UK and around the world. Countries where sexual behaviour is more strictly controlled seem to have fewer cases of AIDS. More isolated communities also seem to have fewer people with AIDS.

THINK

1 What is the best way to avoid contracting AIDS?
2 What does the spread of AIDS tell us about life in the twentieth and twenty-first centuries?
3 Why do you think there is a 'World AIDS Day' and a 'World Cancer Day'?

Reactions to AIDS

The speech bubbles below illustrate some of the ways in which people have reacted to the spread of AIDS.

> AIDS is God's punishment to us for our sinful behaviour and sinful lifestyles.

> If we repent our sins we will be cured.

> People suffering from AIDS should be isolated from the community so that they are unable to harm others.

> AIDS can be caught by touching others.

THINK

1 Look back to people's views on the Black Death and cholera. What are the similarities and differences between people's reactions to these diseases and to AIDS?

2 Make a list of the *similarities* between AIDS and the other epidemics you have studied.

3 Make a list of the *differences* between AIDS and the other epidemics.

4 Compare the two lists. What conclusions can you draw?

Other people have shown compassion, and have set up charities both to treat victims and to try to find a cure. Governments and international organisations like the World Health Organization have spent millions of pounds on awareness campaigns in attempts to slow the spread of the disease. Given this range of responses, have our attitudes to disease changed all that much over the last 1,000 years?

AIDS is seen as a modern-day equivalent of the Black Death, cholera or Spanish Flu, spreading remorselessly across the globe, leaving millions dead in its wake. But is that really the case? What could you do to stop catching the Black Death, or cholera, or the Spanish Flu? Not a lot. These epidemics were no respecter of age, class or sex. AIDS is *different*. It is spread in a clearly identifiable way which can be avoided. Some people argue that there is no *need* for anyone to catch AIDS. If you like, it is a 'lifestyle choice' to behave in a way that makes catching the infection more likely. Also, we know how to stop AIDS spreading. In 1918, 1831–32, or 1348 no one had the faintest idea how to stop those epidemics from becoming so deadly.

Some people see the story of AIDS as a pessimistic one. New diseases and epidemics are always going to break out, and science and technology are not always going to be able to control them. Some people paint an 'apocalyptic' picture of the end of the world where society is wiped out by epidemics.

Others see AIDS in a more optimistic light. Yes, it is an epidemic that has killed millions but governments and international organisations are working hard together to control the spread of the disease and will find a cure. Why do you think we have chosen to use the story of AIDS as a final case study in this book?

Are people healthier now than ever before?

FOCUS TASK

What would happen to you if you fell ill today?

Now it's time to review your work on healthcare in twentieth- and twenty-first-century Britain.

Below in the left-hand column you will find a list of ailments common in the twentieth century. All you have to do is decide how those ailments would be treated, by whom and what the likely outcomes might be.

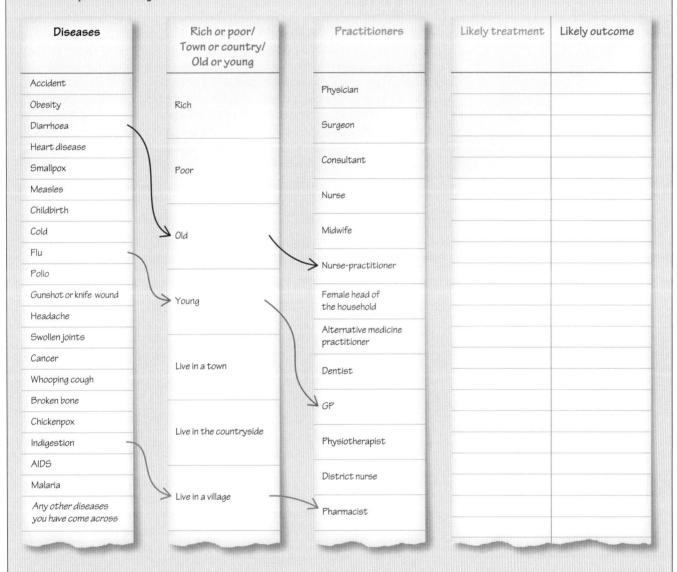

Diseases	Rich or poor/ Town or country/ Old or young	Practitioners	Likely treatment	Likely outcome
Accident		Physician		
Obesity	Rich			
Diarrhoea		Surgeon		
Heart disease				
Smallpox	Poor	Consultant		
Measles				
Childbirth		Nurse		
Cold	Old	Midwife		
Flu		Nurse-practitioner		
Polio				
Gunshot or knife wound	Young	Female head of the household		
Headache		Alternative medicine practitioner		
Swollen joints				
Cancer	Live in a town	Dentist		
Whooping cough				
Broken bone		GP		
Chickenpox				
Indigestion	Live in the countryside	Physiotherapist		
AIDS		District nurse		
Malaria				
Any other diseases you have come across	Live in a village	Pharmacist		

1 Were some diseases more deadly than others?
2 Is this similar to your list for 1900 (page 72), or different?
3 Were some diseases easier to control in the twentieth century than previously?
4 Was medical treatment, in your opinion, any better in 2000 than it had been in 1900? Or in 1600? Or in 1000?

Which factors inhibited or encouraged medical change at this time?

The title of this chapter is 'Modern medicine'. In it you have studied the different ways of treating disease, improvements in surgery, and finally the way both government and individuals responded to the challenges of an unhealthy population. There are still issues over the availability of treatment, equal access to treatment, and whether while some diseases have been overcome, new ones will continue to appear.

FOCUS TASK

Twentieth-century factor card

Throughout your course you have been thinking about how the following factors affected the story of Health and the People. Which of these factors were significant in the last 100 years or so? We think at this time that the role of government has been perhaps the most significant factor for change. But surely, so too has war. And of course we mustn't forget science and technology – and even the role of the individual! Do you agree with our assessment of the causes of change, or do you have your own suggestions?

TWENTIETH-CENTURY BRITAIN		
Factor	Relative importance of the factor	Positive or negative influence
War	4	+++
Superstition and religion		
Chance		
Government	5	+++
Communication		+++
Science and technology	4	+ and −
The economy		
Ideas		
Role of the individual	4	++

1 On your own copy of the factor card decide which factors you think are most important in explaining any changes in health that took place during the twentieth century. Give each factor a number value, where 1 is least important, and 5 most important. Remember to decide whether they are important for creating change, or for inhibiting change. In some cases, it might be both. You need to be able to explain *why* you think some factors were more important than others. Discuss your findings in groups. Do other people in your group agree with your ideas?
2 Can you establish one factor as being clearly more important than others? Perhaps you need to consider different parts of the twentieth century, rather than the period as a whole? One factor might be more important before 1950, perhaps, and others more important after. *How* do you decide?

KEY WORDS

Make sure you know what these words mean, and are able to use them confidently in your own writing. See the Glossary on pages 111–112 for definitions.
- Cloned
- Holistic medicine
- Orthodox medicine
- Pandemic
- Respite care
- Welfare State

CONCLUSION AND REVIEW

FOCUS

While studying this unit you have explored three main areas: medicine, surgery and public health. Each is an integral part of healthcare. Now it is time to step back a little and try to think about the changes you have studied: what they were, what brought them about and what impact they have had on people's lives.

Medicine

The story of medicine through time is one of continuity and of great change. You have studied the way diseases themselves have changed through history, the different people who have been involved in dealing with diseases and the different treatments they have used to do this.

THINK

Study Sources 1 and 2.

1 What do these two images tell us about the role of women in medicine throughout this period?
2 Which other women figure in this book?
3 Why do you think so few women are mentioned?

SOURCE 1

Woman collecting herbs for medicine, from a medieval manuscript

SOURCE 2

Elizabeth Garrett Anderson, the first woman to qualify as a doctor in Britain

ACTIVITY

Medicine through time

Gather all of your 'What happened if you fell ill in …' activity tables together from the Focus Tasks. To start with make some comparisons between medicine in medieval times and medicine today.

1 What were the killer diseases of medieval times? How has that changed today?
2 Who would treat sick people in medieval times? And whose job is that today?
3 How effective was medicine in medieval times? And how effective is it today?

Get together in small groups to try to spot some overall trends in the story of medicine through time.

4 Can your group agree on the top five changes in medicine over the whole period?
5 What do you think is the biggest change? Why?
6 When was there most change in medicine? Can you explain why?
7 Now look at the similarities in medicine through time. What stayed the same?
8 When was there least change in medicine? Can you explain why?
9 Now write three paragraphs to summarise the way that diseases, practitioners and treatments have changed and remained the same, throughout history.

Surgery

Although we know that successful surgery dates from as early as the Stone Age, we also know that surgery has evolved dramatically over time. As well as different surgical procedures, different knowledge and skill requirements and different technology, people have also come up with different ways to deal with pain both during and after surgery.

ACTIVITY

The history of surgery through time

Gather all of your 'What happened if you fell ill in …?' activity tables together from the Focus Tasks.

Using the information you have gathered, put together a PowerPoint presentation entitled 'The history of surgery through time'. Make sure you cover the following points in your presentation:
- Successful surgery dates from as early as the Stone Age.
- What you think has been the biggest change in surgery.
- Whether all changes brought about immediate improvement.
- When the biggest changes occurred, and why.

Use images from this book and your own research, to illustrate your presentation.

ACTIVITY

Room in the balloon?

Below is a list of some of the most significant individuals in the history of surgery. Decide, as a class, if there is anyone you would add to this list.

Significant individuals in the world of surgery
John Arderne – first English surgeon (page 17)
James Simpson – pioneer of anaesthetics (pages 60–61)
Ambroise Paré – pioneered use of ligatures to stop bleeding (page 32)
Alexander Gordon – reduced infection by washing (page 46)
William Cheselden – did quick operations before the days of anaesthetics (page 37)
Harold Gillies – pioneer of plastic surgery (page 82)
Joseph Lister – pioneer of antiseptics (page 62)
Archibald McIndoe – improved skin grafting (page 83)

These individuals are all standing in a hot-air balloon, but there is only space for three of them! The three who get to stay are those who made the most significant contributions to improving surgery. It is your job, as a class, to determine who stays in the balloon.
- Each group should choose one individual and put together a two-minute presentation on their contribution to improving surgery and why they deserve a space in the balloon.
- Once each presentation has been heard, the class should hold a vote to determine who should be thrown out of the balloon!

Changes in public health

The role of government in public health has undergone a huge change over the last 300 years, and we now live in a society in which government is at the heart of healthcare provision. But is it still the case that we should rely on government to provide this?

ACTIVITY

When was there most change in public health?

Look back at the images of London from 1347 to 1935 (pages 22–23, 38–39, 64–65 and 90–91).

1 In groups, make a list of the main changes that have taken place in public health over these years.
2 When was there most change in public health?
3 When was there the least change in public health?
4 Can you explain why in each case?

1347

1665

1848

1935

Government responses

How would the Government respond to the next pandemic?

Throughout history there have been a number of pandemics in Britain. Look back to pages 27, 47, 67, 71, 80 and 95 to see how government responded to:

- the Black Death
- the Plague
- cholera and typhoid
- Spanish Flu
- AIDS.

In small groups work through the following activities:

1 Note down the differences between the ways in which government responded to each of the pandemics listed.
2 Now note down the similarities.
3 Research what bird flu is and how people catch it. How do you think government would react to an outbreak of bird flu in today's society? Consider how the government could learn from previous epidemics and how they were dealt with.
4 What measures might government take to prevent its spread?
5 Write an article from the Government about how people should take action to avoid the disease.

Black Death

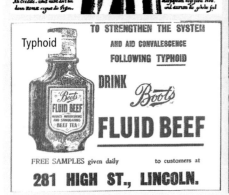
Plague

Typhoid

TO STRENGTHEN THE SYSTEM
AND AID CONVALESCENCE
FOLLOWING TYPHOID
DRINK Boots
FLUID BEEF
FREE SAMPLES given daily   to customers at
281 HIGH ST., LINCOLN.

Spanish Flu

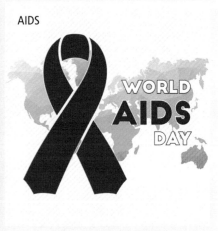
AIDS

Have medical professionals always welcomed change?

While some people always seem to embrace change, others seem to fear it. There have been many instances throughout history where people have been reluctant to make changes, sometimes through fear of change, sometimes because they wanted more evidence of the change being effective, and sometimes because of VESTED INTERESTS.

1 Think of a recent change in your own life and how you responded to it.
2 Now look through your work and list four situations where people were reluctant to embrace a medical change.
3 What do these changes have in common?
4 Why was there resistance to change in each case?
5 What impact did the resistance have on health in each case?
6 Why do you think some changes in medicine were easier to implement than others?

Why do people still fall ill?

During this course, you have discovered many reasons why people fall ill. The diagram below will help remind you of some of them. We're sure you can add more of your own!

Four Humours out of balance

Accident

A home visit from your doctor

Bad air

Refusing to be vaccinated

Unhealthy lifestyle

Inherited from parents

Sin

Epidemic

The planets

God

Bad living conditions

Bad working conditions

Germs

Someone puts a spell on you

Surgery goes wrong

1 In groups, sort the reasons people become ill into four piles:
   a) medieval
   b) early modern
   c) nineteenth century
   d) twentieth century.
2 Each pile corresponds roughly to one chapter of this book. Reasons might appear in more than one pile! You need to agree among yourselves which reason goes in which pile.
3 What do you notice about each pile? Is the twentieth-century list shorter than earlier lists, or longer? Why do you think this is? Does this help you understand some of the changes that have taken place in 'Health and the People'?

Why do people still die of ill-health?

Fewer people die of illness these days than in earlier times, but then you would expect that to be the case, wouldn't you? There has been so much progress in medicines available to treat illness, in the knowledge and skill of surgeons, even in the conditions people live and work in. The whole theme of this book has been medical progress, sometimes faster; sometimes slower; but definitely progress in both prevention and cure. People do live longer (see page 5) but some diseases refuse to be conquered. The epidemics of older times seem to be a thing of the past: the MMR vaccination, polio vaccination, better food, warmer houses, and clean water have seen to that. But other diseases seem to have taken over: previously, few people died of cancer or heart disease (or perhaps they were just not recorded as such!). Now they are the leading cause of death and we are bombarded with requests for money from charities trying to find cures for these deadly diseases. Can science and technology beat disease?

THINK

Will disease always kill people, or might there come a time when everyone can live a long, healthy life?

Drawing conclusions

You now need to reach your own conclusions about Health and the People.

ACTIVITY

Something signficant happened in the story of Health and the People on each date listed below.

1 Check back through the book to identify what happened on each date.
2 Draw your own timeline and arrange the events (with their dates):
   • **above** the timeline if you think they led to positive change
   • **below** the timeline if you think they achieved little or no change, or had a negative impact.
3 This book has been about Health and the People in Britain since around AD1000. There is an assumption that this has been a time of progress, but is that the case? You should now be in a position to decide the answer for yourself.

1000	1665	1847	1918–19
1123	1741	1848	1928
1277	1753	1852	1948
1348	1796	1854	1951
1350	1811	1858	1967
1536	1831–32	1865	1978
1629	1837	1871	1981
1653	1842	1909	1996

Factors for change

The following table shows you where you have studied each of the factors for change throughout the book.

	Topic number																	
Factor	1.1	1.2	1.3	1.4	1.5	2.1	2.2	2.3	2.4	3.1	3.2	3.3	3.4	4.1	4.2	4.3	4.4
War			x											x	x		
Superstition and religion		x	x		x												
Chance											x			x			
Government				x			x	x			x	x		x	x	x	
Communication		x				x	x			x		x	x		x		x
Science and technology			x			x		x		x	x	x	x		x		x
The economy					x						x			x	x	x	x	x
Ideas		x		x		x		x	x		x	x	x		x	x	x
Role of the individual	x	x				x	x	x		x	x	x			x	x	

Gather together all of the factor cards that you created on pages 29, 50, 73 and 98.

1 In small groups study each of your cards and discuss the trends you can see that show different factors being important at different periods of time.
2 Now decide which factor has been the most important in creating change across the whole of your course.

MEDIEVAL BRITAIN

Factor	Relative importance of the factor	Positive or negative influence
War		
Superstition and religion	5	+ and −
Chance		
Government		
Communication		
Science and technology		
The economy		
Ideas		
Role of the individual		

EARLY MODERN BRITAIN

Factor	Relative importance of the factor	Positive or negative influence
War		
Superstition and religion		
Chance		
Government		
Communication		
Science and technology	5	+
The economy		
Ideas		
Role of the individual		

NINETEENTH-CENTURY BRITAIN

Factor	Relative importance of the factor	Positive or negative influence
War		
Superstition and religion		
Chance		
Government		
Communication		
Science and technology		
The economy		
Ideas		
Role of the individual	5	+

TWENTIETH-CENTURY BRITAIN

Factor	Relative importance of the factor	Positive or negative influence
War	4	+++
Superstition and religion		
Chance		
Government	5	+++
Communication		+++
Science and technology	4	+ and −
The economy		
Ideas		
Role of the individual	4	++

ASSESSMENT FOCUS

Britain: Health and the People: c1000 to the present day

How the thematic unit will be assessed

This thematic unit will be examined in the first part of Paper 2 (the second part will be on your chosen British depth studies). The questions could be on any part of the thematic content so you need to know it all.

There are FOUR questions you will need to answer on this part of the paper, focusing on:

● AO1: demonstrate knowledge and understanding of the key features and characteristics of the period studied.
● AO2: explain and analyse historical events and periods studied using second-order historical concepts.
● AO3: analyse, evaluate and use sources (contemporary to the period) to make substantiated judgements, in the context of historical events studied.

| Question | Type | Marks | | | | |
		AO1	AO2	AO3	SPaG	Total marks
1	How useful			8		8
2	Explain significance	2	6			8
3	Compare	4	4			8
4	Factors	8	8		4	20

Remember to refer to AQA's full mark scheme. This can be found on their website.

Using exam questions for revision

When you are revising it is sometimes a good idea to attempt an exam question, before you then re-read the relevant section in the textbook. You don't need to write the answer in full before you re-read the text. You could plan an answer, or draw up a spider diagram or list of ideas. The important thing is to try very hard to remember – before you check what you have done. Once you have re-read the relevant section of the textbook then you should try to write a full answer.

The exam questions

Question 1

Question 1 will ask you to look at a source, and decide how useful it is for a very particular enquiry. The source might be a visual (for example a cartoon or photo) or a written source (for example, a letter or diary). The source might come from any part of the course and deal with any event, development, individual or group.

> 1. Study Source A. How useful is Source A to a historian in explaining why surgery was so dangerous in the fourteenth century?
>
> Explain your answer using Source A and your own contextual knowledge. (8 marks)

SOURCE A

A medieval doctor cutting open a patient's skull with a hammer and blade. An illustration from a fourteenth-century French medical manuscript by Guy of Pavia

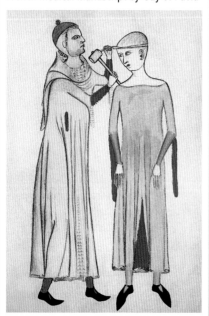

To answer this type of question you will need to use the content of the source – what does the source tell us about medieval surgery? – but also the context and provenance of the source, as well as your own knowledge in order to evaluate how useful this source is in helping to answer the specific question, i.e. why surgery was so dangerous.

This source goes some way to helping us understand why surgery was so dangerous in the fourteenth century.

The content of the source shows a surgeon at work – the patient standing up, no protective clothes, no anaesthetics, simple tools. The provenance tells us this source was published in a medical textbook in the fourteenth century, so is meant as an instruction manual for surgeons, so we can assume it reflects practice at the time. The context, that it was published in Paris, helps because Paris was an important university for the study of medicine at this time.

I know that the Catholic Church, which believed the main way to cure sickness was by prayer and restricted the education of surgeons by both sticking to Galen's ideas and limiting autopsy, made it difficult for surgeons to gather sufficient knowledge of the human body to be effective. But then again we know that surgeons like John Arderne in England were developing effective surgical techniques for some operations.

In conclusion, this source helps us to understand that surgeons were carrying out surgery in the fourteenth century, even if many were not very successful because of their limited knowledge.

- This answer addresses some really important points, on both sides of the question – things that make the source useful but also less useful.
- The answer uses contextual knowledge to highlight the inadequacies of the source as well as its strengths.

OVER TO YOU

Write two more sentences that explore the dangers of surgery in the fourteenth century in more detail.

Question 2

Question 2 will ask you to explain the significance of an event, in the context of a particular enquiry. It might be an event from any of the sections of the course.

2. Explain the significance of anaesthetics in the development of medicine. (8 marks)

To answer this type of question you will need to know about the part anaesthetics played in making surgery safer, as well as more recent twentieth-century developments. You will need to select your examples carefully to make a coherent answer.

You might explain how the use of anaesthetics was viewed critically in some periods and much more positively in others. There were however still critics in the positive periods. What reasons did they cite to justify pain in the Crimea war for example? There are plenty of examples to choose from when responding to Question 2, so remember the focus of the question is *significance*.

In the nineteenth century anaesthetics were seen as the answer to a real medical problem, that of making surgery more effective and reducing the mortality rate which often reached 50 per cent.

Some early surgeons like John Arderne in the fourteenth century began to develop their own pain-reducing solutions to anaesthetise patients to allow them to operate. Many quacks also used copious amounts of alcohol and/or opium to deaden pain, often with disastrous results as it was difficult to measure a precise dose. Some surgeons insisted that pain was an important part of surgery – it helped the patient appreciate their efforts. Clearly, lack of effective anaesthetics severely limited the type of operations many surgeons attempted.

This answer discusses the significance of anaesthetics throughout the period covered by the course, and suggests how this changes. It even suggests why there was some initial opposition to the use of anaesthetics. It doesn't explore the difficulties faced by the early adopters of anaesthetics.

Simpson and Lister were the instigators of major change in the nineteenth century. On the one hand, their new anaesthetics, ether and carbolic acid, made surgery safer, as surgeons did not have to rush their work; on the other hand, mortality rates rose with anaesthetics, as surgeons attempted more challenging procedures. The discovery of anaesthetics radically changed medicine.

Perhaps it is the twentieth century in which anaesthetics have had the greatest impact – more careful and controlled dosage has made many tricky operations more routine. An increasingly scientific approach has enabled the anaesthetist to ensure the patient remains comfortable and safe. Increasingly, local anaesthetics have been used for smaller operations – dentistry is a good example where even as recently as the 1960s extraction of teeth was often carried out under a general anaesthetic whereas today a local injection into the gum is sufficient.

In conclusion the development of effective anaesthesia has had a profound impact on both the type of surgery carried out and the survival rates of patients.

OVER TO YOU

To take this further, think about:

- Which powerful groups of people resisted changes in surgery?
- Which factors, other than anaesthetics, played a part in the development of better surgery? Perhaps the answer needs to explore the role of the individual a little.
- You might explore how the significance of something can change over time.

Question 3

Question 3 will ask you to compare two key events. Again, they might be from any part of the course. The comparison will usually be in terms of similarity not difference.

3. Compare the Black Death in the Middle Ages with the outbreaks of cholera in the nineteenth century. In what ways were they similar? (8 marks)

Obviously you need to know about the Black Death and cholera to be able to answer this type of question. You also need to know about life in the fourteenth century and in the nineteenth century (i.e. the wider context).

Let's take the Black Death first. Where did it come from? What did people think caused it? How did they treat it? What was its impact on society? Did they come close to deciding either the cause or an effective treatment? Similarly, for cholera: What did people think caused it? How did they respond to it? How did they 'cure' it, and what was its impact?

One possible approach to answering this type of question could be to focus on each disease in turn then draw a conclusion. Another way to highlight similarities would be to write a series of paragraphs to compare, in turn, their causes, then their impact, then treatments. Whatever approach you choose remember that all good history writing needs a clear conclusion to pull your arguments together.

There is lots of debate about the Black Death, and especially its causes. Where did it come from? What did people think caused it? How did they treat it? What was its impact on society?

We do know that people knew the pestilence was coming, and that many people would die. What they couldn't agree on was how to cure it. Attempts to cure it show the inadequacies of medieval medicine. And yet there were some attempts to isolate victims and clean up towns. The main focus was on prayer and flagellation – begging forgiveness for bad behaviour. Its impact was huge, with some communities losing perhaps 75 per cent of their population. Altogether, it is thought that around 40 per cent of the population of England died during the Black Death.

Cholera, too, had a huge impact, especially in London, and attempts to deal with it were in some ways very similar to the way the Black Death was treated, but with less emphasis on religion and more on practical measures such as removing dirt and smells. Again, people knew that cholera was spreading along trade routes, but remained hopeful it was the 'Asiatic Flu' or the 'English Diarrhoea'. The 1848 outbreak was directly responsible for the 1848 Public Health Act.

These events are similar in that people initially didn't know or understand either what caused them, or how to cure people from them, although John Snow's work shows the impact of scientific investigation in dealing with disease. They are also similar in that they both continued to revisit England after their initial impact.

> - This answer emphasises the similarities between the two key events. It uses some contextual knowledge of both medieval and Victorian society and the issues involved, for example by mentioning dirty towns, to explore the similarities. However it does not focus in enough detail on attempts to deal with either disease.
> - The answer could have included more about the cures people tried.
> - It could have mentioned specific examples.

OVER TO YOU

Find out more about the causes and cures for both epidemics from this book and then add more detail to this answer.

Question 4

Question 4 is worth nearly half the total marks for this section of the paper. It requires a 'big picture' knowledge of the whole course. To answer this type of question you need to produce a sustained argument that makes a coherent whole and which clearly answers the question. The question will focus on the factors for change that are central to the course:

- War
- Superstition and religion
- Chance
- Government
- Communication
- The economy
- Ideas
- Science and technology
- The role of the individual in encouraging or inhibiting change

> 4. Has the role of the individual been the main factor in the development of medicine in Britain since medieval times? Explain your answer with reference to the role of the individual and other factors. (16 marks plus 4 marks for Spelling, Grammar and Punctuation)

This is an essay so remember to structure your answer carefully and to focus on the question which asks about *the role of the individual in advancing medicine since medieval times* and *other factors*. You will be aware of many individuals who advanced medicine and individuals whose ideas and status eventually restricted progress. When it comes to 'other factors' you have plenty of evidence in your factor charts to show that it was not just about individuals. Pick good examples and explain them clearly, then reach a clear conclusion.

There are plenty of examples we could use to show how important the individual has been in advancing medicine – Vesalius, Paré, William Harvey, Jenner, Chadwick, Fleming or Beveridge are just a few. There are other individuals whose influence might be seen to limit the development of medicine – Galen being an example.

Jenner and the spread of vaccination against smallpox is perhaps the best example, as this had an immense impact. Despite opposition, despite being ignored as a 'country doctor', Jenner persevered and made a huge impact on medicine post 1800 – arguably more than any other individual. We could probably make the same claim for Koch, or Fleming, or Barnard and his pioneering work on transplants. Perhaps it is fair to say that the individual has had more impact in the second part of the period we have studied than the first part.

This answer focuses very clearly on the question. The first section picks out several individuals who have made major changes in medicine, and uses some across the breadth of the course. The third paragraph picks out one individual who might have held back progress, *and explains why.*

The next section then picks out other factors for change – not all the factors studied during the course, but many of them.

- The whole answer is carefully planned and structured.
- A conclusion, which could be stronger, attempts to pull this all together. Various examples are used; perhaps more could have been used from later in the course.

We ought also to mention Galen as an individual with a negative influence, and his role in limiting progress in the Middle Ages, as the Church accepted his beliefs without question and thus made it difficult to carry out autopsies and thus discover the exact workings of the human body.

It is important to emphasise other factors, too, in the development of medicine. War has been especially important, with Vesalius and Paré learning new techniques while serving with the army, and of course the work of pioneer surgeons during the First and Second World Wars. We have already referred to science in answer 2, and also the role of the Church – sometimes encouraging change, as in setting up universities and medical schools, and sometimes limiting change, as in its strict adherence to Galen and the belief in prayer as a way to cure illness.

What is clear is that the development of medicine is complicated, with no one factor in itself responsible for change. Sometimes chance is important – Fleming's accidental discovery of penicillin for example – but more often it is a combination of factors that lead to major developments. Fleming may have discovered penicillin, but it was both the work of Florey and Chain, and of course the demands of the Second World War, and the role of big business, that led to its successful commercial application.

In conclusion, individuals have had a major impact on the development of medicine over time, but they are far from the only factor involved.

OVER TO YOU

- Use the textbook and/or your revision notes to pull together some supporting detail for the individuals you have used in your answer.
- Use the textbook and/or your revision notes to find examples of people from earlier in the course that you might include in your answer.
- Consider if your answer contains enough 'other factors' to effectively answer the question.

Keys to success

As long as you know the content and have learned how to think, these exams should not be too scary. The keys to success are:

- **Read the question carefully.** This may sound obvious, but there is a skill to it. Sometimes students answer the question they wish had been asked rather than the one that has actually been asked. So identify the skill focus (what they are asking you to do). Do they want you to write a description, an explanation or a comparison? Identify the content focus (what it is about) and select knowledge that will help you answer the question that has been asked.
- **Note the marks available.** That helps you work out how much time to spend on answering each question. Time is precious. If you spend too long on low-mark questions you will run out of time for the high-mark ones.
- For essays in particular, **plan your answer before you start writing.** Know what you are going to say; then write clearly and logically. Leave a little time to check your work. You are unlikely to have time in an exam to actually rewrite an answer, but you can check for obvious spelling mistakes, missing words or other writing errors that might cost you marks.

GLOSSARY

ALMSHOUSES: Houses paid for and built by someone, often a charity, where poor people, mainly the old or the sick, can live when they are unable to work

AMPHIBIAN: Animal that lives on land and in water, like a frog or newt

ANAESTHETIC: A substance that stops a patient feeling pain

ANTICYCLONE: A high pressure weather system that often brings very still air conditions

ANTISEPTIC: Something that stops disease-spreading organisms growing and spreading in the body

ASCLEPION: Ancient Greek temple of healing – the equivalent of our hospitals

ASEPTIC: Sterile, or totally free from contamination by viruses or disease-spreading organisms

AUSTERITY: Time when government spends as little money as possible, in order to help the economy grow. Usually means less spending on services like education, health, house-building

AUTOPSY: The opening up of a corpse to try to find out why a person has died

BACILLUS: Bacteria that cause disease

BIOLOGICAL WARFARE: Using toxins or disease-carrying infections to wage war. The Japanese tested plague, smallpox and cholera on Chinese prisoners during the Second World War to try to develop a bomb to drop on California

CAPILLARIES: Very fine blood vessels for taking the blood around the body

CAUTERISE: Burn the skin or flesh of a wound with a heated instrument or caustic substance in order to stop bleeding or to prevent infection

CESSPIT: A pit or hole in the ground to dispose of sewage

CLASSICAL: Ancient Greek or Roman

CLONING: Copied exactly

COMPENSATE: Pay money to make up for a mistake or injury

COMPULSORY: Have to do something; you have no choice in the matter

DESTITUTE: Without money, food or a home

DOCTRINE OF SIGNATURES: States that herbs that resemble various parts of the body can be used by herbalists to treat ailments of those parts of the body. The doctrine dates from Galen's time

DUNGHILL: A heap of waste left to rot

EFFLUENT: Liquid waste discharged into a river or sea

EMBRYO: Unborn baby

EMETIC: Something taken to make you vomit or be sick with the aim of removing impurities from your system

EMPIRICISM: Belief that all knowledge comes from observation, from experimental science

ENDEMIC: A disease regularly found in that part of the country/world

ENTREPRENEUR: Someone who invests money to build a factory or mill, in order to make themselves a lot of money if they are successful

EPIDEMIC: A sudden, widespread occurrence of an infectious disease

GELATIN CAPSULES: Virtually colourless and tasteless water-soluble protein used to deliver carefully controlled doses of a medicine. Used as an alternative to tablets

GREENFIELD SITE: One not built on before; has usually been farmland previously

HEREDITY: The passing on of genetic characteristics by parents to children

HIPPOCRATIC OATH: Oath taken by new doctors agreeing to do no harm to their patients. Still widely used today by new doctors

HOLISTIC MEDICINE: Looking at and treating the body as a whole

HOLY LAND: Jerusalem and the area around it that was and still is sacred to Christians. The Crusades were an attempt to recapture it from the Muslims who controlled it, and also think of it as 'holy'

HYPOCHONDRIA: Thinking one is always ill

IMMUNE: Not at risk from catching that particular disease or infection

INDULGENCE: If you bought an Indulgence from the Church, the Church would lessen the punishment for your sins, allowing you to get to Heaven quicker once you died

INEXORABLY: Inevitably

INFANT MORTALITY: The number of children who die, usually measured per thousand of the population – for example, infant mortality might be 100 per thousand

INHERITANCE: Money left to you by parents, grandparents etc. or, in this case, for a special purpose

INOCULATION: Early form of vaccination where the skin is scratched rather than injected

ISSUES: The practice of making holes in the body to let out noxious matter

LAISSEZ-FAIRE: A belief that some things were not the job of government, but should be 'left alone' or left to individuals to do for themselves

LATRINE: Toilet

LICENSEE: Someone given permission to make and sell something by the owner – in this case a German firm let a British company make and sell thalidomide in return for payments to the German firm

LIFE EXPECTANCY: How long, on average, people might expect to live

LIGATURE: A cord used to tie something very tightly, in this case in order to stop bleeding

MALNOURISHMENT: Not enough to eat

MORTALITY: Death rate, usually measured per thousand of the population

NATIONALISATION: Take over something by government, so government runs the service, factory or industry

ORTHODOX MEDICINE: Conventional medicine

PANDEMIC: Disease covering a huge area or the whole world

PHYSIC GARDEN: Garden used solely for growing herbs used in preparing medicines and treating illnesses

POULTICE: A soft, moist mass of material, often made from bran, flour, herbs, etc., applied to the body to relieve soreness and inflammation and kept in place with a cloth

PRIVATE PATIENTS: Patients who pay their doctor to be treated

PRIVY: Toilet

PURGATORY: Christians believe that when you die you go to Heaven if you have been really good, or Hell if you have been really bad. Purgatory is where you go if you are in between, until you have paid for your sins and then can go to Heaven. That is why many people bought indulgences – to shorten their time in Purgatory

RESPITE CARE: Somewhere for terminally ill patients to go for a period of time, to give their family or carers a chance to live a 'normal' life for a while

SCROTAL CANCER: Cancer of the testicles, or scrotum

SECULAR: Not to do with religion

SERUM: Part of the blood that can be separated out and used to provide immunity from a specific disease

STERILE: Free from bacteria or other living microorganisms; totally clean

STERILISATION: Operation that prevents people from having children

TRANQUILLISERS: A medicine or drug taken to reduce tension or anxiety

VACCINATION: Injection of a mild form of disease to stop you getting a more dangerous version of the disease

VESTED INTEREST: A personal reason for doing something, especially an expectation of financial or other gain

WELFARE STATE: Where government looks after people, takes responsibility for education, medicine, etc. Paid for by taxes rather than by the individual. Introduced by the Labour Government after the Second World War

INDEX